Andreas Geiger

Probabilistic Models for 3D Urban Scene
Understanding from Movable Platforms

Schriftenreihe
Institut für Mess- und Regelungstechnik,
Karlsruher Institut für Technologie (KIT)
Band 025

Eine Übersicht über alle bisher in dieser Schriftenreihe erschienenen
Bände finden Sie am Ende des Buchs.

Probabilistic Models for 3D Urban Scene Understanding from Movable Platforms

by
Andreas Geiger

Dissertation, Karlsruher Institut für Technologie (KIT)
Fakultät für Maschinenbau
Tag der mündlichen Prüfung: 19. April 2013
Referenten: Prof. Dr. Christoph Stiller, Prof. Dr. Raquel Urtasun

Impressum

 Scientific
Publishing

Karlsruher Institut für Technologie (KIT)
KIT Scientific Publishing
Straße am Forum 2
D-76131 Karlsruhe

KIT Scientific Publishing is a registered trademark of Karlsruhe
Institute of Technology. Reprint using the book cover is not allowed.

www.ksp.kit.edu

Print on Demand 2013

ISSN 1613-4214
ISBN 978-3-7315-0081-0

Probabilistic Models for 3D Urban Scene Understanding from Movable Platforms

Zur Erlangung des akademischen Grades

Doktor der Ingenieurwissenschaften

der Fakultät für Maschinenbau
des Karlsruher Instituts für Technologie (KIT)
genehmigte

Dissertation

von

DIPL.-INFORM. ANDREAS GEIGER

aus Kirchheim unter Teck

Tag der mündlichen Prüfung: 19. April 2013
Hauptreferent: Prof. Dr. Christoph Stiller
Korreferent: Prof. Dr. Raquel Urtasun

Für meine Frau Anja und
meine Eltern Walburga und Günter

Vorwort

Die vorliegende Arbeit entstand während meiner Tätigkeit als wissenschaftlicher Mitarbeiter am Institut für Mess- und Regelungstechnik am Karlsruher Institut für Technologie (KIT) unter Prof. Christoph Stiller.

Zunächst möchte ich mich herzlich bei Herrn Prof. Christoph Stiller für die Anregung zu dieser Arbeit, die wissenschaftliche Förderung und für die Übernahme des Hauptreferates bedanken. In gleichem Maße gilt mein Dank meiner Korreferentin Prof. Raquel Urtasun, welche mich seit meiner Diplomarbeit wissenschaftlich betreut, gefördert und zu neuen Ideen inspiriert hat. Gerne erinnere ich mich zurück an unsere gemeinsame Zeit in Lausanne, Boston und Chicago. Prof. Marc Pollefeys danke ich für die Möglichkeit drei Monate an der ETH Zürich zu forschen und neue Einblicke in die Welt der 3D Rekonstruktionen zu gewinnen.

Dr. Martin Lauer danke ich für die Entführung in die Zauberwelt der Samplingverfahren. Zudem bedanke ich mich bei allen Mitarbeitern des Institutes für Mess- und Regelungstechnik sowie bei Alexander Schwing und Roland Angst für die wissenschaftlichen Diskussionen, die entstandenen Freundschaften und die fröhlichen Momente bei Geburtstagen, Einstandsfeiern, Sommerseminaren, Sportveranstaltungen und Skiausflügen.

Des Weiteren bedanke ich mich bei unserem Systemadministrator Werner Paal, der Werkstatt und dem Sekretariat des MRT für die stets unbürokratische und freundliche Bearbeitung von Auf- und Anträgen. Den Herren Shaban und Käptn Peng gebührt mein Dank für die musikalisch-philosophische Unterstützung und für den Kreis.

Für die finanzielle Unterstützung danke ich der Deutschen Forschungsgemeinschaft (DFG), der Karlsruhe School of Optics and Photonics (KSOP) und dem Karlsruhe House of Young Scientists (KHYS), welche mir Forschungsprojekte und Auslandsaufenthalte ermöglicht haben.

Zum Schluss möchte ich mich bei meinen Eltern bedanken, die mich in jeder Hinsicht förderten, mir ein sorgenfreies Studium ermöglicht haben und jederzeit für mich da waren. Aus tiefstem Herzen danke ich meiner Frau Anja für ihre Geduld während arbeitsintensiven Phasen ("Deadlines"), ihr Verständnis und die Motivation, ohne die diese Arbeit nicht möglich gewesen wäre.

Karlsruhe, 2013   *Andreas Geiger*

Zusammenfassung

Visuelles 3D Szenenverständnis stellt eine wichtige Komponente für automatisiertes Fahren und die Navigation von Robotern dar. Innerstädtische Kreuzungsszenarien sind hierbei in gleichem Maße interessant wie auch anspruchsvoll: Straßenkreuzungen können komplexe Geometrien annehmen und oft werden wichtige Hinweise auf die Geometrie, wie zum Beispiel Fahrbahnmarkierungen oder andere Verkehrsteilnehmer, durch Objekte im Sichtfeld verdeckt. Während autonomes Fahren auf Schnellstraßen (Dickmanns et al. [51]) sowie das Überqueren einfacher annotierter Kreuzungen (DARPA Urban Challenge [31]) bereits erfolgreich gezeigt wurde, bleibt die Behandlung des allgemeinen innerstädtischen Falls mit geringem Vorwissen auch weiterhin ein ungelöstes Problem. Diese Arbeit stellt einen Beitrag zum Verständnis von Verkehrsszenen basierend auf Videosequenzen dar. Ein auf dem Dach des Versuchträger AnnieWay [106] angebrachtes Kamerasystem liefert die dafür benötigten Sensorinformationen. Vorgestellt wird ein probabilistisches generatives Modell, welches die 3D Szenengeometrie sowie die Position und Orientierung von Objekten in der Szene schätzt. Insbesondere werden die Topologie, Geometrie sowie Aktivitäten der Verkehrsteilnehmer aus kurzen Videosequenzen bestimmt. Das Verfahren zieht dabei monokulare Informationen wie Objekte, Fluchtpunkte sowie eine semantische Bildsegmentierung als Merkmale heran. Zusätzlich wird der Einfluss stereoskopischer Merkmale wie Szenenfluss und Belegungsgitter untersucht. Motiviert durch die beeindruckende Fähigkeit des Menschen wird kein weiteres Wissen wie beispielsweise GPS-, Lidar-, Radar- oder Karteninformationen vorausgesetzt. Die auf 113 repräsentativ ausgewählten Sequenzen durchgeführten Experimente zeigen dass der vorgestellte Ansatz für eine Vielzahl von

Szenarien geeignet ist. Eine umfangreiche Auswertung und Analyse gibt Aufschluss über die Relevanz der einzelnen Merkmale. Des Weiteren wird aufgezeigt, wie durch das vorgeschlagene Verfahren eine verbesserte Objektdetektion und -orientierungsschätzung erreicht werden kann.

Abstract

Visual 3D scene understanding is an important component in autonomous driving and robot navigation. Intelligent vehicles for example often base their decisions on observations obtained from video cameras as they are cheap and easy to employ. Inner-city intersections represent an interesting but also very challenging scenario in this context: The road layout may be very complex and observations are often noisy or even missing due to heavy occlusions. While Highway navigation (e.g., Dickmanns et al. [51]) and autonomous driving on simple and annotated intersections (e.g., DARPA Urban Challenge [31]) have already been demonstrated successfully, understanding and navigating general inner-city crossings with little prior knowledge remains an unsolved problem. This thesis is a contribution to understanding multi-object traffic scenes from video sequences. All data is provided by a camera system which is mounted on top of the autonomous driving platform AnnieWAY [106]. The proposed probabilistic generative model reasons jointly about the 3D scene layout as well as the 3D location and orientation of objects in the scene. In particular, the scene topology, geometry as well as traffic activities are inferred from short video sequences. The model takes advantage of monocular information in the form of vehicle tracklets, vanishing lines and semantic labels. Additionally, the benefit of stereo features such as 3D scene flow and occupancy grids is investigated. Motivated by the impressive driving capabilities of humans, no further information such as GPS, lidar, radar or map knowledge is required. Experiments conducted on 113 representative intersection sequences show that the developed approach successfully infers the correct layout in a variety of difficult scenarios. To evaluate the importance of each feature cue, experiments with different feature combinations are conducted. Additionally, the proposed method is shown to improve object detection and object orientation estimation performance.

Contents

Notation and Symbols

This chapter introduces the notation and symbols which are used in this thesis. In cases where a symbol has more than one meaning, the context (or a specific statement) resolves the ambiguity.

General Notation

Scalars	Regular (greek) lower case	a, b, c, σ, λ
Vectors	Bold (greek) lower case	$\mathbf{a}, \mathbf{b}, \mathbf{c}, \boldsymbol{\sigma}, \boldsymbol{\lambda}$
Matrices	Bold upper case	$\mathbf{A}, \mathbf{B}, \mathbf{C}, \boldsymbol{\Sigma}, \boldsymbol{\Lambda}$
Sets	Calligraphic upper case	$\mathcal{A}, \mathcal{B}, \mathcal{C}$
Distributions	Calligraphic upper case	$\mathcal{U}(\cdot),\quad \mathcal{N}(\cdot), \mathcal{C}at(\cdot)$
Numbers	Blackboard/greek upper case	$\mathbb{N}, \mathbb{Z}, \mathbb{R}, \Delta$

Indexing

i	First-order index $i \in \{1, \ldots, N\}$
j	Second-order index $j \in \{1, \ldots, M\}$
a_i	i'th element of vector $\mathbf{a}$
$A_{i,j}$	(i, j)'th element of matrix $\mathbf{A}$
$[\mathbf{a}_1, \mathbf{a}_2]$	Matrix $\mathbf{A} = [\mathbf{a}_1, \mathbf{a}_2]$ is composed of columns $\mathbf{a}_1$ and $\mathbf{a}_2$

Numbers

$\mathbb{N}$	Natural numbers
$\mathbb{Z}$	Integer numbers
$\mathbb{R}$	Real numbers
Δ^N	N-simplex

Geometry

$\mathcal{R}$	Intersection parameters $\mathcal{R} = \{\kappa, \mathbf{c}, w, r, \alpha\}$
κ	Intersection topology $\kappa \in \{1, \ldots, 7\}$
$\mathbf{c}$	Center of intersection $\mathbf{c} \in \mathbb{R}^2$
w	Road width $w \in \mathbb{R}^+$
r	Road layout orientation $r \in [-\frac{\pi}{4}, +\frac{\pi}{4}]$
α	Crossing street angle $\alpha \in [-\frac{\pi}{4}, +\frac{\pi}{4}]$
l	Lane index
s	Spline index
K	Number of intersection arms $K \in \{2, 3, 4\}$
L	Number of lanes/parking spots

Image Evidence

$\mathcal{E}$	Image evidence $\mathcal{E} = \{\mathcal{T}, \mathcal{V}, \mathcal{S}, \mathcal{F}, \mathcal{O}\}$
$\mathcal{T}$	Tracklets $\mathcal{T} = \{\mathbf{t}_1, \ldots, \mathbf{t}_{N_t}\}$
$\mathbf{t}$	Tracklet $\mathbf{t} = \{\mathbf{d}_1, \ldots, \mathbf{d}_{M_d}\}$
$\mathbf{d}$	Detection $\mathbf{d} = (f_d, \mathbf{m}_d, \mathbf{S}_d, \mathbf{o}_d)$
f_d	Frame number of object detection $f_d \in \mathbb{N}$
$\mathbf{m}_d, \mathbf{S}_d$	Object location distribution $\mathcal{N}(\mathbf{m}_d \in \mathbb{R}^2, \mathbf{S}_d \in \mathbb{R}^{2 \times 2})$
$\mathbf{o}_d$	Object orientation distribution $\mathbf{o}_d \in \Delta^7$
$\mathcal{V}$	Vanishing points $\mathcal{V} = \{v_1, \ldots, v_{N_v}\}$
v	Vanishing point/line angle $v \in [0, \pi)$
$\mathcal{S}$	Scene labels $\mathcal{S} = \{\mathbf{s}_1, \ldots, \mathbf{s}_{N_s}\}$
$\mathbf{s}$	Scene label $\mathbf{s} \in \Delta^2$
$\mathcal{F}$	Scene flow $\mathcal{F} = \{\mathbf{f}_1, \ldots, \mathbf{f}_{N_f}\}$
$\mathbf{f}$	Scene flow vector $\mathbf{f} = (\mathbf{p}_f, \mathbf{q}_f)$, $\mathbf{p}_f \in \mathbb{R}^2$, $\mathbf{q}_f \in \mathbb{R}^2$
$\mathcal{O}$	Occupancy grid $\mathcal{O} = \{o_1, \ldots, o_{N_o}\}$
ρ	Occupancy grid cell $\rho \in \{-1, 0, +1\}$

Projection

$(x, y, z)^{\mathsf{T}}$	World coordinates
$(u, v)^{\mathsf{T}}$	Image coordinates
$\boldsymbol{\pi}(\cdot)$	Projection onto the image plane

$\mathbf{K}$	Camera calibration matrix $\mathbf{K} \in \mathbb{R}^{3\times3}$ (intrinsics)
$\mathbf{P}$	Camera projection matrix $\mathbf{P} \in \mathbb{R}^{3\times4}$
$\mathbf{R}$, $\mathbf{r}$	Rotation matrix, rotation vector
$\mathbf{T}$, $\mathbf{t}$	Translation matrix, translation vector
$\mathbf{I}$	Image
$\mathbf{D}$	Disparity map

Probabilistic Model

Θ	Model parameters
$\mathcal{E}$, $\mathcal{R}$	Training set ($\mathcal{E} = \{\mathcal{E}_1, .., \mathcal{E}_D\}$, $\mathcal{R} = \{\mathcal{R}_1, .., \mathcal{R}_D\}$)
$p(\cdot)$	Probability
$\log p(\cdot)$	Log-probability
$\phi(\cdot)$, $\varphi(\cdot)$	Image likelihood helper functions
$\psi(\cdot)$, $\Psi(\cdot)$	Potential functions
ζ, λ	Image likelihood outlier and importance variables
σ_{out}	Standard deviation of outlier distribution
$q(\cdot)$	Metropolis-Hastings proposal distribution
$p_{MH}(\cdot)$	Metropolis-Hastings acceptance probability
$\mathcal{U}(\cdot)$	Uniform distribution (discrete or continuous)
$\mathcal{N}(\cdot)$	Gaussian distribution
$\mathcal{C}at(\cdot)$	Categorical distribution
μ, $\boldsymbol{\mu}$	Mean
σ^2, $\boldsymbol{\Sigma}$	Variance, covariance matrix
λ, $\boldsymbol{\Lambda}$	Precision $\lambda = \sigma^{-2}$, precision matrix $\boldsymbol{\Lambda} = \boldsymbol{\Sigma}^{-1}$
$\langle\cdot\rangle_{p(\cdot)}$	Expectation with respect to $p(\cdot)$
$[\cdot]$	Iverson bracket (1 if true, 0 otherwise)

Notation of Probability Distributions

This thesis follows the common notation of probability distributions and uses $p(x) = \mathcal{D}(x|\theta)$ and $x \sim \mathcal{D}(\theta)$ interchangeably, where x is a random variable, $\mathcal{D}$ denotes some probability distribution and θ are the parameters of the distribution.

1. Introduction

Recent progress in self-driving vehicles makes us believe that only a few decades from now drivers can be replaced by autonomous systems that excel humans in terms of perception (e.g., omni-directional sensors), availability and the ability to respond. Improved safety and time for work and leisure activities while traveling are the consequence. While vehicle control and trajectory planning algorithms have already been demonstrated successfully, robust environment perception is still a challenging unsolved problem. This thesis presents a method to extend the vehicle's field of view to the challenging scenario of cluttered real-world intersections while relying solely on close-to-production stereo image sensors.

1.1. Problem Statement

Given a short traffic video sequence of 5 to 30 seconds in length captured from a movable platform we are interested in extracting information about the scene layout and the dynamic objects, e.g., vehicles, present in the scene. In particular, we tackle traffic scenarios with complex interactions. They pose an interesting problem and are challenging due to the heavy occlusions and the clutter present in these scenes. Additional difficulties are caused by the low camera viewpoint leading to noisy depth estimates and the limited camera field of view. In particular, the proposed method tries to answer the following questions:

- Where are the streets and the center of the intersection located?

- What is the width and the orientation of the streets?

- Where are the vehicles located and how are they oriented?

- Which car is driving? On which street?

- Which cars are parked at the side of the road?

- What is the current traffic situation?

- Does object detection benefit from the extracted road layout?

We try to answer the aforementioned questions from visual measurements alone, which are easy and cheap to acquire, never get outdated (as maps do) and mimic the human perception process. All sequences used for evaluation end when the observer is required to take a decision, i.e., when the traffic light turns green or the ego-vehicle enters the crossing. This requires predicting into the future and makes the task very challenging. Much like for human drivers no additional information such as 3D point clouds from a laser scanner, radar or maps is used.

While the problem of lane detection has been tackled intensely over the last decades [4, 44, 51, 137, 173, 185], the detection and recognition of lane markings in isolation is not sufficient to infer the scene layout in complex situations. Consider for example the scene illustrated in Fig. 1.1, where all non-road pixels of the image have been whitened. Even for a human being it is almost impossible to judge the situation using lane markings as the only source of information. In contrast, Fig. 1.2 reveals the full picture and shows that a variety of feature cues are important to understand the scene *in context* [179]. Amongst them are: Other traffic participants, buildings, vegetation, vanishing points and the sky region. Drawing from these observations, this thesis combines a variety of features in a probabilistic framework to tackle the problem as illustrated in Fig. 1.3(b).

1.2. Applications

We highlight three important applications of traffic scene understanding.

Figure 1.1.: Intersection from a Lane Detector's Point of View. This figure shows a typical traffic scene with all non-road pixels masked. Note how difficult it is to correctly assess the intersection geometry using this information alone. To see the full picture, please turn over to Fig. 1.2 on page 4.

Autonomous Driving: While the total number of fatal traffic accidents has been slightly decreasing over the last couple of years, in 2010 still more than 12,000 fatalities have been reported in the US[1] and more than 3,500 cases have been registered in Germany[2]. The ultimate goal of autonomous driving is to substitute the human driver with an intelligent system which is able to process the incoming sensor information and react appropriately in order to maneuver the vehicle from A to B. However, autonomous driving has the potential to significantly reduce traffic accidents [138] and vehicle emissions [187] at the same time, for example by increasing roadway capacity and reducing traffic jams [146]. As a side effect, passengers gain additional time which can be utilized for work or leisure activities. So far, autonomous driving has been successfully demonstrated on highways with little or no traffic. Busy inner-city navigation, however, is still an open challenge.

Advanced Driver Assistance Systems: While autonomous driving at large scale might still be decades away, many research find-

---

[1] National Highway Traffic Safety Administration Facts Sheet 2010
[2] Statistisches Jahrbuch 2011

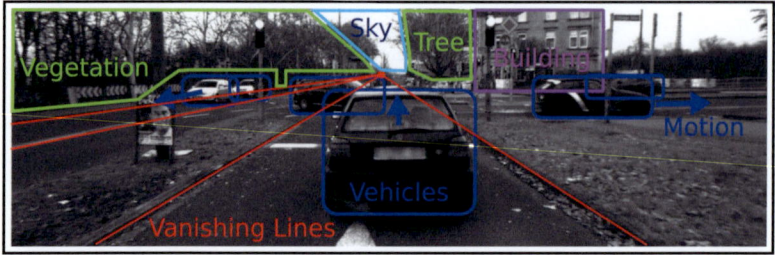

Figure 1.2.: **Intersection from a Human's Point of View.** To interpret complex scenes as the one from Fig. 1.1 on page 3, humans make use of a variety of different cues such as infrastructure (e.g., buildings or vegetation), vanishing points, objects and dynamic information. The presented approach builds on this observation and integrates the different complementary features into a probabilistic model for analyzing traffic scenes.

ings have already made their way into commercial driver assistance systems such as lane departure warning [127], automatic parking or collision avoidance [189]. Visual scene analysis at intersections can add to these functionalities by warning the driver of overlooked traffic participants or when entering the wrong lane. Furthermore, navigation systems will benefit from the extracted 3D information by enhancing their visual experience and simplifying the interaction with the user.

Visually Impaired People: Traffic scene understanding is of high importance for blind people as well, for example the situation must be assessed correctly before to crossing the street [1]. Today's assistance is typically provided by short-range white canes or guide dogs which both can only be employed for navigating known terrain [52]. Computer-based scene analysis in combination with visualization techniques such as acoustic auralization [182] has the potential to increase the range of perception, contribute to a higher quality of life and increase safety.

1.3. Contributions

The contributions of this thesis are as follows:

- A novel intersection model is proposed which, in contrast to existing lane or road detection methods, is flexible in the number of intersecting streets and the location, orientation and width of the intersection arms.

- Compared to existing approaches, no static camera, bird's eye view or information from maps is required.

- In contrast to previous approaches, the proposed model combines static features (e.g., building facades or vanishing points) with dynamic features (e.g., traffic participants) for improved performance and robustness.

- Efficient learning and inference algorithms based on Markov Chain Monte Carlo sampling and belief propagation are developed to infer the scene layout and the location of objects within the scene.

- Extensive evaluations on 113 real-world sequences demonstrate the applicability of the method and confirm that context helps in scene estimation as well as object recognition. The importance of each of the proposed feature cues for the problem of 3D scene understanding is evaluated and discussed.

1.4. Thesis Outline

This thesis is structured as follows: Chapter 2 surveys the current state-of-the-art and contrasts the proposed approach with respect to previous work. Chapter 3 presents the proposed geometric and probabilistic intersection model and the parameter learning and model inference techniques that are employed. Chapter 4 gives details about the image evidence and the computation of the features used by the

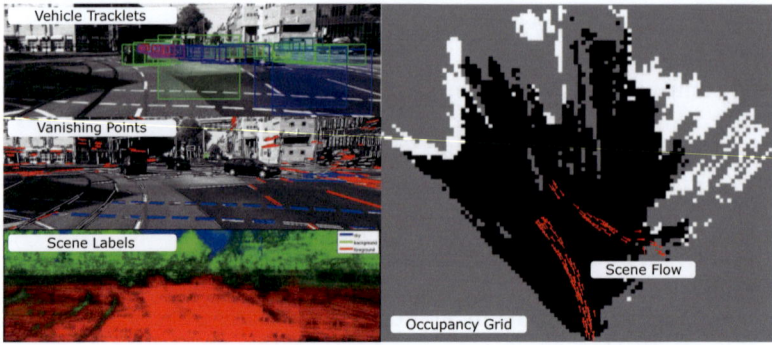

(a) Video-based Image Cues are the Input to the Proposed Model

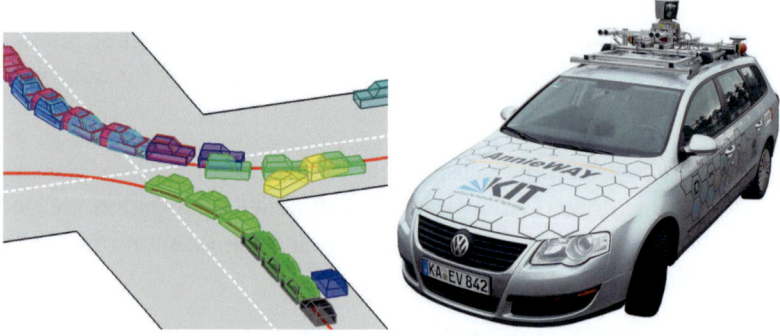

(b) Inference Result: Scene Layout and Objects   (c) Experimental Platform AnnieWAY

Figure 1.3.: **3D Intersection Understanding.** (a) Image cues. (b) Inferred scene layout and objects, active lanes are shown in red. (c) Autonomous vehicle AnnieWAY which has been used for capturing the evaluation sequences.

model. Finally, Chapter 5 describes the autonomous platform, the data collection process and the experiments that have been carried out. Conclusions are drawn in Chapter 6. A brief tutorial on the sampling techniques that we use for learning and inference is given in Appendix A.

2. Related Work

This chapter discusses the state-of-the-art in autonomous driving systems and scene understanding, and positions the contributions of this thesis with respect to the existing literature, summarized in Fig. 2.1. We start with an overview of the development of autonomous driving systems, survey their capabilities and current challenges.

2.1. Autonomous Driving

In 1939 General Motors invited the industrial designer Bel Geddes to submit a proposal for an exhibit at the New York's World Fair 'Building The World of Tomorrow'. The exhibit, called 'Futurama', envisioned a world 20 years into the future featuring automated highways as a solution to traffic congestion of the day. Electric cars were powered by circuits embedded in the roadway and controlled by radio, much like modern production lines work today. In 1986, supported by the rapid development of computers, a team of engineers around Ernst Dickmanns in collaboration with Daimler equipped a Mercedes-Benz van with cameras and successfully demonstrated the first self-driving car on well-marked streets without traffic [51]. Subsequently, the European Commission began funding the EUREKA Prometheus Project on autonomous vehicles (1987–1995). In 1995 the team demonstrated semi-autonomous driving in real traffic from Munich in Germany to Odense in Denmark at speeds up to 175 km/h, with human intervention for about 5% of the distance. At the same time, the CMU Navlab project achieved 98.2% autonomous driving with manual longitudinal control using the RALPH (Rapidly Adapting Lateral Position Handler) computer program [152]. Similar efforts have been undertaken in 1996 and 2010 by the research group of Alberto Broggi [28], amongst others. In 2011, the Grand Co-operative Driving Challenge has benchmarked the state-of-the-art in autonomous platooning systems with Christoph Stiller's Team An-nieWAY from KIT taking the lead [68].

All aforementioned projects are targeted at tasks like highway driving, lane-keeping/-following or overtaking. In contrast, this thesis deals with the more challenging task of understanding traffic situations at intersection, which are much more flexible in terms of topology, geometry and vehicle constellation.

2.1.1. The DARPA Urban Challenge

Motivated by the success of the Grand Challenges in 2004 and 2005 [30], the American Defense Advanced Research Projects Agency initiated the DARPA Urban Challenge [31, 106, 139, 100] in 2007 to benchmark the state-of-the-art in autonomous inner-city driving on a 96 km test course at an abandoned Air Force Base. As for the previous challenges and in contrast to the early approaches mentioned above, 100% autonomous driving was required throughout the course.

While the Urban Challenge endeavor came closer to urban traffic situations, the streets were wider than usual, the field of view was unobstructed and only a very limited number of traffic participants were present. Furthermore, sub-meter precise manually annotated maps were required and all teams made use of expensive 3D laser scanner equipment for localization and collision avoidance. In contrast, the approach presented in this thesis aims at analyzing complex and cluttered scenes in the absence of maps or 3D point clouds.

2.1.2. The Google Driverless Car

Under the guidance of Sebastian Thrun, Google gathered a team of engineers, amongst them Chris Urmson (the current team lead), Mike Montemerlo and Anthony Levandowski who had experienced the DARPA Grand [30] and Urban [31] Challenges, to equip a Toyota Prius with self-driving capabilities [188]. In August 2012 Google announced that they have completed over 300,000 miles without accident.

Similarly to the participants of the DARPA Urban Challenge, the Google driver-less car is equipped with a Velodyne 3D laser scanner for perception and requires manually annotated maps at lane-level accuracy for path planning. Furthermore, its precise localization system is based on registering depth and reflectance measurements with respect to a 3D map, which is recorded a-priori. In contrast, this thesis targets scene understanding in the more general and challenging case where no a-priori location-specific information is required.

2.2. Environment Perception

One major challenge for intelligent autonomous driving systems is the requirement to perceive and interpret their environment. We focus on cheap and easy-to-employ video-based perception and this section surveys the current state-of-the-art in this field. The spectrum of the referenced works ranges from very task-specific methods (e.g., lane detection) to more general scene understanding approaches (e.g., scene segmentation and 3D interpretation).

2.2.1. Lane Detection

The pioneering works of Dickmanns et al. [51] made use of an extended Kalman Filter [105] to recursively estimate lane parameters such as the steering angle, slip angle, lateral offset from the road center, heading relative to the road tangent and the horizontal and vertical road curvature parameters. The road was represented using a clothoid (or Euler spiral) which is commonly employed in road planning and construction. As features, edge elements were extracted by correlating the image with filter templates. Besides modeling the road shape with clothoids [51, 45, 176], splines [4, 16, 45, 36] have

9

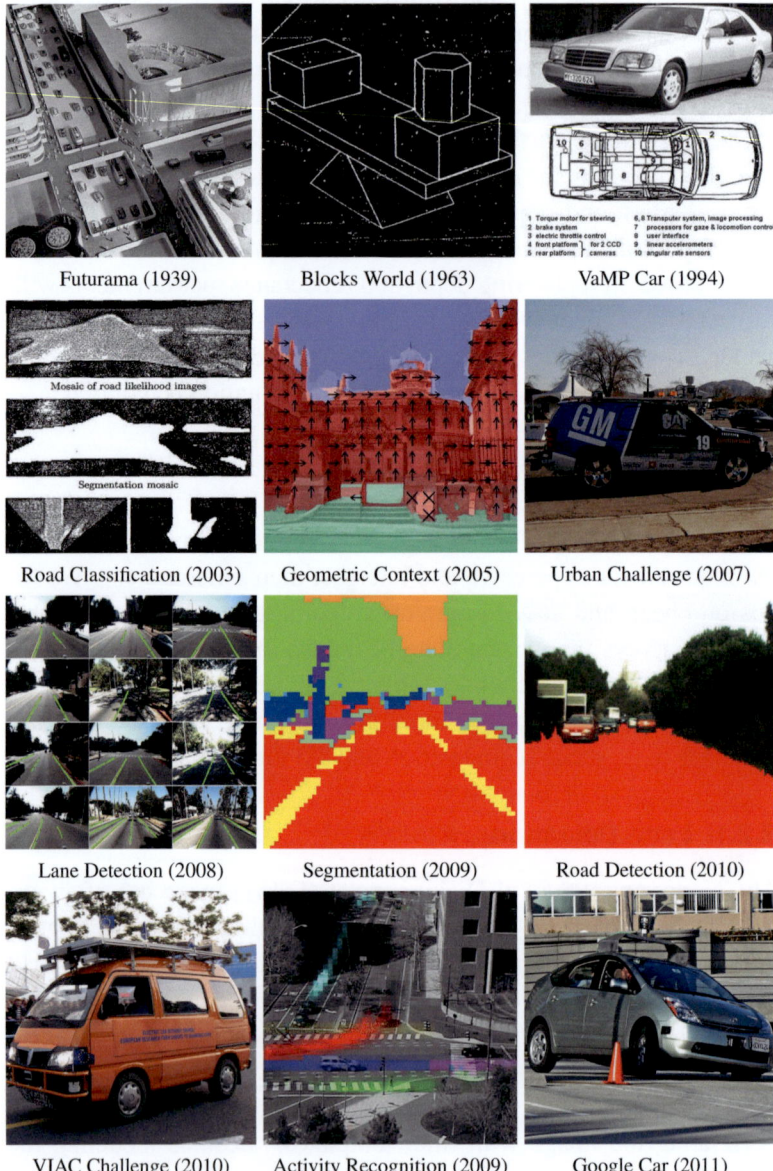

Figure 2.1.: **Related Work** in autonomous driving/environment perception.

been proposed to more accurately represent road segments that do not obey a clothoidal shape. Apart from edge features, other cues such as color, lane width [8, 44] and adaptive binarization techniques [55, 27] have been investigated. In order to remove the effect of distortions introduced by the perspective projection, the inverse perspective mapping has been proposed [27, 4, 66], constructing a virtual bird's eye view of the road area ahead of the vehicle by means of the homography between the road and the image plane. Due to the increase in computing power over the last decades, the extended Kalman filter has been replaced by the more powerful particle filter [44, 173, 185] for tracking the road parameters over time. In contrast to the extended Kalman filter no linearization is required and multi-modal distributions can be represented more accurately, given a sufficient number of particles – or equivalently – computation time. To distinguish lane markings from clutter such as cast shadows and damages in the road surface, robust methods have been developed [4, 8, 185]. Furthermore, the use of stereo information has been reported to additionally boost performance [16, 45, 44, 111, 177, 186] as it enables distinguishing edge information on the road from edges located on objects and infrastructure. While early stereo-based approaches applied the idea of Helmholtz shear [111] for computational reasons, recent progress in dense real-time stereo matching [113, 64, 93, 133, 73] allows to directly estimate the free space and segment road from objects and infrastructure [10, 12, 11] in an online fashion. Paetzold et al. [147] have cast lane recognition as an optimal control problem where the vehicle trajectory is directly optimized to avoid obstacles and maximize comfort at the same time. The use of maps has been investigated bei Heimes, Huang et al. [90, 100]. They map line segments into the image using GPS as initialization to improve localization accuracy [90]. Furthermore, map information in combination with a precise GPS system have been key to successful navigation during the DARPA Urban Challenge [100]. For a more complete survey on recent developments in lane detection, the reader is referred to [107, 137].

While all of the methods mentioned above focus on the detection of one to three adjacent lanes, this thesis is concerned with the intersection scenario and handles lane detection as a subset of intersection understanding.

2.2.2. Road Detection

While lane detection approaches try to fit parametric models to the lane boundaries, methods for road detection are non-parametric in the sense that they directly produce a segmentation of the image into road and non-road pixels. This is useful in cases of less structured roads, for example when driving on dirt roads as required during the DARPA Grand Challenge [30]. Early approaches directly classify each pixel using the gray value structure tensor as feature [199]. To increase robustness, different cues such as color, vanishing points and the 3D scene layout have been proposed and integrated over time [3]. Online learning approaches [2, 42] inspect a small road patch in front of the vehicle, e.g., identified by lidar [42], to learn a statistical model of the road ahead and classify image regions further away. According to Dahlkamp et al. [42], such a mechanism turned out to be key for increasing the range of vision in order to drive fast enough to win the 2005 DARPA Grand Challenge.

All state-of-the-art road detection methods focus on recognizing a single road and work well in unstructured terrain where texture and color are discriminative enough to distinguish road from vegetation or background. As will be shown in this thesis, texture based classification alone, which is one of the features in our framework, is insufficient for extracting higher-level information about intersections such as the topology or geometry.

2.2.3. Intersection Recognition

Back in the early 1990's the problem of intersection understanding has been recognized as a difficult one [41, 56, 77]. In the case of unstructured terrain, pattern recognition techniques have been employed to partition the image into road and non-road pixels and classify the shape of the road using template matching [41] or classification [154, 58]. To increase the field of view, active camera vision systems have been proposed [104, 136]. For well marked roads, Enkelmann et al. [56] aim at recovering gaps between road markings as indications of intersections. Gengenbach [77], Heimes [89, 90] and Mueck [140] project intersection models, which have been manually annotated or obtained from maps [29] in a semi-supervised fashion, into the image in order to localize the vehicle when the approximate location is known up to a couple of meters. Richer prior knowledge has been incorporated into these methods using description logic. In [102, 103], for example, a description logic base for arbitrary road and intersection geometries has been developed. Based on map information, logically stated geometric constraints and road building regulations are employed in a deductive inference scheme to answer questions like 'is this lane a right turn lane?' or 'which lane is the vehicle on?'.

All existing methods deal with very simple scenarios, neglecting clutter and occlusions, or require an immense amount of labor intense prior knowledge. This prevents them from being employed to real-world urban traffic situations. We argue that road and lane features by themselves are insufficient to robustly infer the road layout. Instead a more diverse set of feature cues such as the scene flow fields induced by other participants [67], infrastructure elements [69], vanishing points and scene labels [74] need to be considered in order to accomplish the task.

2.2.4. Semantic Image Segmentation

While the approaches described so far are largely rooted in the domain of robotics and intelligent vehicles, the perceptual side of scene understanding has received a lot of attention in the computer vision and machine learning communities as well. In the following, we in-

13

troduce the most important developments in these fields and relate the material presented in this thesis with respect to them.

The goal of semantic image segmentation [118, 117, 58, 174, 9, 203, 54, 21, 63, 81, 83, 83, 120, 170, 170, 181, 191] is to partition the input image into disjoint regions and assign a unique class label (e.g., car, building, vegetation or sky) to each of them. Contextual information is typically integrated by means of a Markov random field model.

While these models reason directly at the pixel-level, they provide useful cues which are exploited as features in the proposed approach. We aim to infer the full 3D layout of traffic intersections from a monocular view including the accurate position of buildings, the street and all vehicles.

2.2.5. 3D Indoor Scene Understanding

Several decades after Roberts first attempts [155] in 1963, the problem of 3D scene understanding has witnessed novel interest thanks to the developments in object detection, semantic segmentation and image classification, amongst others. A wide variety of approaches have been proposed to recover the 3D layout of *indoor* scenes in the form of 3D cuboids from a single image [126, 87, 183, 125, 168]. These methods mainly build on edges and image segments as features, and most of them rely on the Manhattan world assumption [114, 157], i.e., edges in the image can be associated with vanishing points which are orthogonal to each other. With a moderate degree of clutter, accurate geometry estimation has been shown for this scenario. To improve performance, several methods have tried to explicitly model the room clutter using 3D occupancy grids [87] or cuboids [88, 149, 125, 195]. Recently, depth information from the Kinect sensor has been explored towards the goal of estimating support relationships between objects [171]. Context from observing people and their interaction with the environment has been investigated by Breitenstein, Delaitre et al. [25, 49] and a vertical structure prior has been proposed by Zeisl et al. [198].

Unfortunately, these approaches can only cope with limited amounts of clutter (e.g., beds), and rely on the fact that indoor scenes closely satisfy the Manhattan world assumption, i.e., walls (and objects) are aligned with the three dominant vanishing points. In contrast, outdoor scenes as considered in this thesis are often more cluttered, 3D lines are not necessarily orthogonal [166, 15], and objects might not always agree with the dominant orientations.

2.2.6. 3D Outdoor Scene Understanding

Apart from the efforts towards geometric multi-view reconstruction [128, 40, 151] for urban scenes, a large body of work has focused on estimating 3D popups from single images captured *outdoors* [96, 94, 97, 98, 163, 161, 162, 164, 91, 142]. Often a Manhattan world [15, 114, 157] is assumed to infer vanishing points from line segments. Reminiscent to the Blocksworld model, physical constraints between objects such as 'object A supports object B' are imposed in [84]. Large datasets such as LabelMe [160] allow for similarity-based scene understanding [159], where ground truth labels are transferred from the most similar scenes in the database. Several methods have tried to infer the 3D locations of objects in outdoor scenarios [95, 14, 50]. In order to estimate 3D object locations, tree-structured models have been proposed [95, 14] which also reason about the camera tilt. Murphy et al. [141] exploit object co-occurrence statistics to improve object detection, while Sudderth at al. [175] make use of hierarchical Dirichlet processes to model visual scenes. The most successful approaches use tracklets to prune spurious detections by linking consistent evidence in successive frames [108, 101, 65]. However, these models are either designed for static camera setups in surveillance applications [101] or do not provide a rich scene description [108, 65]. Notable exceptions are [37, 57, 190, 192, 193], which jointly infer the camera pose with respect to a single ground plane and the location of objects in the scene. Unfortunately, most urban scenes violate the Manhattan world assumption and several approaches have focused on estimating vanishing points in this more adversarial setting [166]. For example, Barinova et al. [15] proposed to jointly perform line detection as well as vanishing point, azimuth and zenith estimation.

Unfortunately, most of the existing 3D scene layout estimation techniques are mainly qualitative, do not model object dynamics, suffer from clutter and lack the level of accuracy necessary for real-world applications such as autonomous driving or robot navigation. Existing methods that take objects into account usually model the scene in terms of a simple ground plane and thus are not able to draw conclusions from the complex interplay of the objects with the larger scene layout. In contrast, we propose a method that is able to extract accurate geometric information by reasoning jointly about static and dynamic elements as well as their interplay. Towards this goal we develop a rich image likelihood model that takes advantage of vehicle tracklets, vanishing points, segmentations, scene flow and occupancy grids.

2.2.7. Object Tracking and Activity Recognition

For a long time dynamic objects have been considered either in isolation [153, 65, 20, 6, 7, 13, 43, 112, 131] or jointly using simple motion models [101, 24, 32, 57, 109, 129, 130, 167, 172, 194, 200, 197, 202]. Only very recently, social interaction between individuals has been taken into account [196, 38, 37, 124]. Choi et al. [38] introduce a hierarchy of activities, modeling the behavior of groups and Pellegrini et al. [148] explicitly account for collisions. Methods for unsupervised activity recognition and abnormality detection [115, 184] are able to recover spatio-temporal dependencies from a static camera mounted on top of a building.

While promising results have been shown, the interplay of objects with their environment is neglected and the focus is put on surveillance scenarios with a fixed camera viewpoint, limiting applicability. In contrast, the method developed in this thesis infers semantics at a higher level such as multi-object traffic patterns at intersections, in order to improve the layout and object estimation processes. Importantly, we do inference over intersections that we have never seen before and our viewpoint is substantially lower compared to the surveillance scenario, which renders the problem very challenging.

3. Urban Scene Understanding

This thesis tackles the problem of estimating complex 3D traffic scenes (e.g., intersections) from video sequences. The sequences have been captured from a moving vehicle as illustrated in Fig. 1.3(c). Here, 2D refers to observations in the image plane and 3D refers to coordinates in bird's eye perspective. We assume a flat road surface and model the scene layout and all objects in the road coordinate system. The road coordinate system is located directly below the left camera in the last frame using the same yaw angle and coordinate axis definition (x = right, y = down, z = forward). All points on the road satisfy $y = 0$. An illustration of the road coordinate system with respect to the camera is given in Fig. 3.1(b) and Fig. 4.3.

3.1. Geometric Model

The proposed model is based on our observation of typical traffic scenes: We assume that the global layout of the scene is dominated by two, three or four roads intersecting at a single point, the center of the intersection. All vehicles are either parked at designated parking areas at the side of the road or they drive on lanes and adhere to some basic traffic rules such as right-hand driving. Lanes are modeled using B-splines and connect every inbound street with every outbound street. Road boundaries determine the border between drivable regions and areas that are likely to contain buildings and infrastructure. We model seven different scene topologies and use the following parameters to describe the intersection:

- **Topology**. The discrete topology variable κ distinguishes between the scene topologies 'straight', 'turn', 'T-intersection' and 'X-intersection' as illustrated in Fig. 3.1(a). $\kappa \in \{1, \ldots, 7\}$.

- **Center of intersection**. The intersection center $\mathbf{c}$ defines the point where all roads join and is specified in terms of the road coordinate system, depicted in Fig. 3.1(b). $\mathbf{c} = (x, z)^\mathsf{T} \in \mathbb{R}^2$.

- **Street width**. As our depth measurements are very noisy and the size of the opposing streets are often not observable, we assume that all streets share the same width w. The consequences of this assumption are analyzed in our experimental evaluation. $w \in \mathbb{R}^+$.

- **Rotation**. The rotation r accounts for the observer's yaw orientation with respect to the incoming street. $r \in [-\frac{\pi}{4}, +\frac{\pi}{4}]$.

- **Crossing angle**. The crossing angle α refers to the relative orientation of the crossing street. Alternate intersection arms are forced to be collinear, which is a reasonable assumption. $\alpha \in [-\frac{\pi}{4}, +\frac{\pi}{4}]$.

All variables are illustrated in Fig. 3.1. In the following they will be subsumed using the road layout variable $\mathcal{R} = \{\kappa, \mathbf{c}, w, r, \alpha\}$.

Lane Model: An important contribution of the proposed model is to account for the interplay of dynamic objects (i.e., vehicles) with their environment (e.g., streets or buildings). This is realized by assuming that, given the road layout, all traffic participants can be explained as either driving on designated lanes, which we model with the help of B-splines, or being parked at a parking area at the side of the road.

For simplicity, we restrict our focus to two lanes per street, one incoming and one outgoing lane for each intersection arm. Streets with multiple lanes can be represented in our model by means of a larger street width w. As vehicles are allowed to cross the intersection in

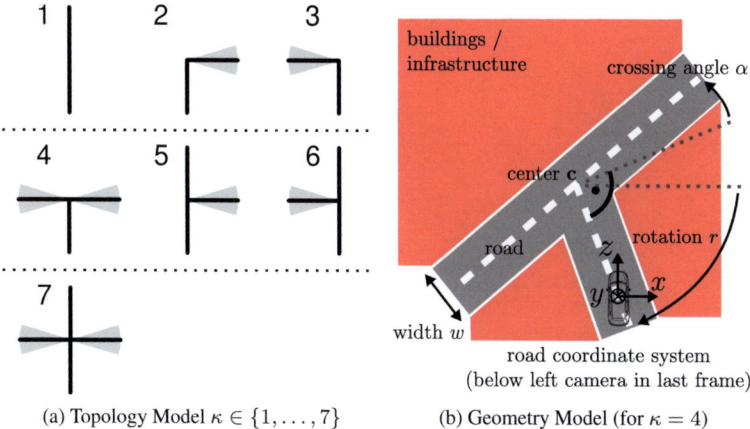

(a) Topology Model $\kappa \in \{1, \ldots, 7\}$ (b) Geometry Model (for $\kappa = 4$)

Figure 3.1.: **Road Topology and Geometry.** (a) shows the 7 different topologies κ we consider: Straights (1), turns (2,3), T-intersections (4-6) and X-intersections (7). The gray shaded areas illustrate the flexibility of the crossing street. (b) shows the geometric parameters of the model for $\kappa = 4$. All modeling is done in bird's eye perspective (road plane coordinates).

any possible direction, we have $K(K-1)$ lanes for a K-armed intersection. For each street we model two parking areas at the side of the road, one at the left side and one at the right side, yielding $2K$ parking areas in total. Two (out of six) lanes of a 3-armed intersection as well as one parking area are illustrated in Fig. 3.2(a).

Lane centerlines are modeled using quadratic B-splines [48] governed by five control points $\{\mathbf{q}_1, \ldots, \mathbf{q}_5\}$ which are located at the center of the lane as illustrated in Fig. 3.2(b), with $\mathbf{q}_3$ the intersection center. Using de Boor's recursion formula [48], a spline can be

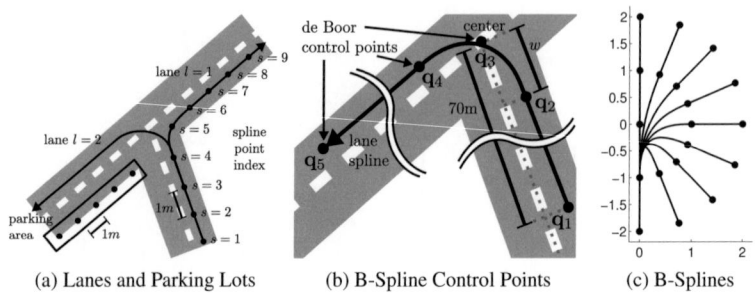

(a) Lanes and Parking Lots   (b) B-Spline Control Points   (c) B-Splines

Figure 3.2.: **Lane Model.** This figure illustrates the location of the lane centerlines with respect to the road layout using B-splines. (a) shows 2 out of 6 lanes and 1 out of 6 parking areas for a 3-armed intersection. All lanes and parking areas are discretized at 1m intervals to facilitate inference. The placement of the 5 control points that define a lane spline is depicted in (b). A set of quadratic B-splines with knot vector $\mathbf{t}$ is illustrated in Fig. 3.2(c).

recursively expressed as

$$\mathbf{s}(t) = \sum_{i=1}^{5} b_{i,2}(t)\mathbf{q}_i$$
$$b_{i,j}(t) = \frac{t - t_i}{t_{i+j} - t_i} b_{i,j-1}(t) + \frac{t_{i+j+1} - t}{t_{i+j+1} - t_{i+1}} b_{i+1,j-1}(t)$$
$$b_{i,0}(t) = [t_i \leq t < t_{i+1}] \tag{3.1}$$

where $t \in [0..1]$ is the curve parameter, t_i is the i'th entry of the knot vector $\mathbf{t}$, $b(t)$ are the basis B-splines, $\mathbf{q}_i \in \mathbb{R}^2$ is the i'th control point as illustrated in Fig. 3.2(b), and $[\cdot]$ denotes the Iverson bracket. The knot vector, controlling the shape of the B-spline through Eq. 3.1, is chosen as $\mathbf{t} = (0\ 0\ 0\ 0.1\ 0.9\ 1\ 1\ 1)^\mathsf{T}$ which forces the spline to interpolate all but the central control point. Empirically this resulted in realistic curvatures as illustrated in Fig. 3.2(c). We refer the reader to [48] for details.

Given all lane splines and all parking areas, we equidistantly define discrete vehicle locations (s) at 1m intervals as illustrated in Fig.

3.2(a). This makes inference very efficient as dynamic programming algorithms can be employed for calculating marginals and MAP estimates. At inference, the vehicle locations are obtained by assigning all detected objects to one of these locations. Note that this assignment links the object detections with the static elements in the scene (e.g., road, buildings, vanishing points).

3.2. Image Evidence

Besides the geometric model, which is entirely determined by the road parameters $\mathcal{R} = \{\kappa, \mathbf{c}, w, r, \alpha\}$, we define a probabilistic model to explain the evidence $\mathcal{E}$ in the image. The observations are collected from a set of monocular and stereo feature cues which we introduce in the following.

First, we detect objects and track them over time, yielding vehicle *tracklets*, which we denote by $\mathcal{T}$. They provide us with information about where the lanes and the parking areas might be located, which are central in our geometric model described in Section 3.1. Furthermore, vanishing points $\mathcal{V}$ give useful hints about the direction of the streets since many scene elements such as road markings or building facades are often aligned with the principal axes of the scene. Segmenting the image into semantic categories $\mathcal{S}$ such as road, background or sky, provides valuable information about the extend of the roads and urban canyons.

In addition to the monocular feature cues described so far, we also leverage low-level stereo features. For instance, 3D scene flow $\mathcal{F}$ is extracted as a cue for moving objects in the scene and an occupancy grid $\mathcal{O}$ provides complementary hints at the location of buildings and infrastructure alongside the road.

We summarize all feature cues as image evidence, denoted by $\mathcal{E} = \{\mathcal{T}, \mathcal{V}, \mathcal{S}, \mathcal{F}, \mathcal{O}\}$, which we will define in the following. For details on the feature extraction pipeline, we refer the reader to Chapter 4.

Vehicle Tracklets: Let $\mathcal{T}$ denote the set of vehicle tracklets $\mathcal{T} = \{\mathbf{t}_1, \ldots, \mathbf{t}_{N_t}\}$ that have been detected in the sequence. A vehicle tracklet $\mathbf{t}$ is defined as a sequence of object detections projected into bird's eye perspective $\mathbf{t} = \{\mathbf{d}_1, \ldots, \mathbf{d}_{M_d}\}$ with $\mathbf{d} = (f_d, \mathbf{m}_d, \mathbf{S}_d, \mathbf{o}_d)$. Here, $f_d \in \mathbb{N}$ is the frame number and $\mathbf{m}_d \in \mathbb{R}^2, \mathbf{S}_d \in \mathbb{R}^{2\times2}$ are the mean and covariance of the Gaussian distribution $\mathcal{N}(\mathbf{m}, \mathbf{S})$ describing the object location in road coordinates. $\mathbf{o}_d \in \Delta^7$ are the parameters of a categorical distribution over eight possible viewpoints (estimated by the object detector) with the unit N-simplex Δ^N defined by

$$\Delta^N = \left\{ \mathbf{x} \in \mathbb{R}^{N+1} \,\middle|\, \sum_{i=1}^{N+1} x_i = 1 \wedge \forall_i: \; x_i \geq 0 \right\} \tag{3.2}$$

Vanishing Points: Furthermore, we detect up to two (N_v) dominant vanishing points $\mathcal{V} = \{v_1, \ldots, v_{N_v}\}$ and represent them by a single rotation angle around the yaw axis of the road coordinate system $v_i \in [0, \pi)$. The vertical vanishing point is non-informative for our task and not considered here.

Semantic Scene Labels: We define the set of semantic labels $\mathcal{S} = \{\mathbf{s}_1, \ldots, \mathbf{s}_{N_s}\}$ by subdividing the image into N_s patches (or 'superpixels') of size $n_s \times n_s$ pixels. For each patch, $\mathbf{s}_i \in \Delta^2$ denotes the discrete probability distribution over the semantic categories *road*, *background* and *sky*. This feature is computed for the last frame in each sequence as this gives us the best possible view at the scene.

Scene Flow: The scene flow $\mathcal{F} = \{\mathbf{f}_1, \ldots, \mathbf{f}_{N_f}\}$ features capture the 3D motion in the scene, compensated for the observer's ego-motion. Each flow vector $\mathbf{f} = (\mathbf{p}_f, \mathbf{q}_f)$ is defined by its location $\mathbf{p}_f \in \mathbb{R}^2$ and velocity $\mathbf{q}_f \in \mathbb{R}^2$ on the road plane. All velocity vectors are normalized to $\|\mathbf{q}_f\|_2 = 1$ as our scene flow model does not explicitly reason about vehicle velocities.

Occupancy Grid: The occupancy grid $\mathcal{O} = \{\rho_1, \dots, \rho_{N_o}\}$ is represented by N_o cells of size $n_o \times n_o$ meters. Each cell $\rho_i \in \{-1, 0, +1\}$ can be either *free* (-1), *occupied* $(+1)$ or *unobserved* (0).

3.3. Probabilistic Model

By assuming all observations $\mathcal{E} = \{\mathcal{T}, \mathcal{V}, \mathcal{S}, \mathcal{F}, \mathcal{O}\}$ to be conditionally independent given the road layout $\mathcal{R}$, the joint distribution over the image evidence $\mathcal{E}$ and the road parameters $\mathcal{R}$ factorizes as

$$p(\mathcal{E}, \mathcal{R}|\Theta) = \underbrace{p(\mathcal{R}|\Theta)}_{\text{Prior}} \underbrace{\left[\prod_{i=1}^{N_t} p(\mathbf{t}_i|\mathcal{R}, \Theta) \right]}_{\text{Vehicle Tracklets}}$$

$$\times \underbrace{\prod_{i=1}^{N_v} p(v_i|\mathcal{R}, \Theta)}_{\text{Vanishing Points}} \underbrace{\prod_{i=1}^{N_s} p(\mathbf{s}_i|\mathcal{R}, \Theta)}_{\text{Scene Labels}}$$

$$\times \underbrace{\prod_{i=1}^{N_f} p(\mathbf{f}_i|\mathcal{R}, \Theta)}_{\text{Scene Flow}} \underbrace{\prod_{i=1}^{N_o} p(\rho_i|\mathcal{R}, \Theta)}_{\text{Occupancy Grid}} \qquad (3.3)$$

where Θ denotes the set of all parameters in our model. This is also illustrated in the graphical model shown in Fig. 3.3.

3.3.1. Prior

The prior on road parameters $\mathcal{R}$ factorizes as

$$p(\mathcal{R}|\Theta) = p(\kappa|\Theta)p(\mathbf{c}, r, w|\kappa, \Theta)p(\alpha|\kappa, \Theta) \qquad (3.4)$$

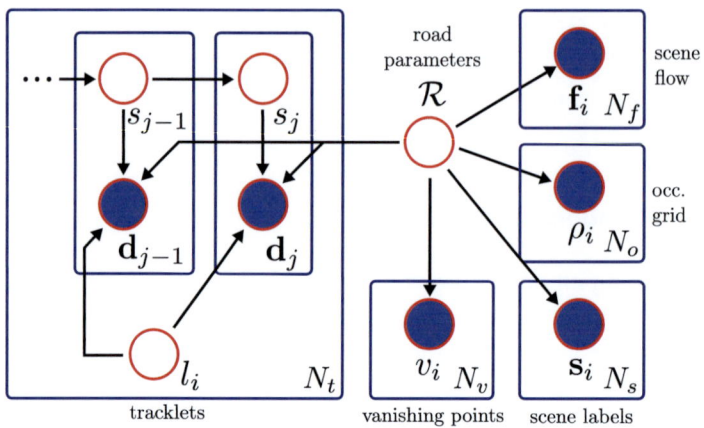

Figure 3.3.: **Directed Graphical Model.** This figure shows the factorization of the joint probability distribution in Eq. 3.3 using a directed graph. Random variables are depicted with circles, observed variables are filled and dependencies between random variables are highlighted using directed arrows. The plate notation is adopted to denote copies.

with

$$\kappa \sim Cat(\boldsymbol{\xi}_p) \tag{3.5}$$

$$(\mathbf{c}, r, \log w)^\top | \kappa \sim \mathcal{N}\left(\boldsymbol{\mu}_p^{(\kappa)}, \boldsymbol{\Lambda}_p^{(\kappa)^{-1}}\right) \tag{3.6}$$

$$\alpha | \kappa \sim f_\kappa(\alpha, \sigma_\alpha)^{\lambda_p} \tag{3.7}$$

where $Cat(\cdot)$ denotes the categorical distribution

$$p(\kappa|\Theta) = Cat(\kappa|\boldsymbol{\xi}_p) = \xi_{p,\kappa} \quad \text{with} \quad \sum_{i=1}^{7} \xi_{p,i} = 1 \tag{3.8}$$

and $\mathbf{c}, r$ and w are modeled jointly to capture correlations between the variables. w is modeled using a log-Normal distribution due to its positivity constraint. Empirically we found α to be highly multi-modal and model it using kernel density estimation $f_\kappa(\alpha, \sigma_\alpha)$

with kernel bandwidth σ_α. All parameters $\boldsymbol{\xi}_p, \boldsymbol{\mu}_p, \boldsymbol{\Lambda}_p, \lambda_p \in \Theta$ are learned from training data using real-world intersections labeled in GoogleMaps aerial imagery as described in Section 5.3. Note that the symmetric positive definite precision matrix $\boldsymbol{\Lambda}_p$ has to be parameterized appropriately. For details on the parameterization and the learning procedure the reader is referred to Section 3.5. The likelihood terms in Eq. 3.3 are described in the following.

3.3.2. Vehicle Tracklets

Recall that a vehicle tracklet $\mathbf{t}$ is defined as a sequence of object detections projected into bird's eye perspective $\mathbf{t} = \{\mathbf{d}_1, \ldots, \mathbf{d}_{M_d}\}$ with object detections $\mathbf{d} = (f_d, \mathbf{m}_d, \mathbf{S}_d, \mathbf{o}_d)$, where $f_d \in \mathbb{N}$ is the frame number, $\mathbf{m}_d \in \mathbb{R}^2, \mathbf{S}_d \in \mathbb{R}^{2 \times 2}$ describe the object location in road coordinates and $\mathbf{o}_d \in \Delta^7$ is the discrete object orientation distribution. Let l be an additional latent variable representing either the lane or the parking area where tracklet $\mathbf{t}$ has been observed as illustrated in Fig. 3.2(a). Assuming a uniform prior on all $K(K-1)$ lanes and all $2K$ parking areas

$$l \sim \mathcal{U}(\{1, \ldots, K(K-1) + 2K\}) \tag{3.9}$$

the tracklet likelihood is defined as the marginal distribution

$$p(\mathbf{t}|\mathcal{R}, \Theta) = \sum_{l=1}^{L} p(\mathbf{t}, l|\mathcal{R}) \tag{3.10}$$

$$p(\mathbf{t}, l|\mathcal{R}) = p(l|\mathcal{R})p(\mathbf{t}|l, \mathcal{R}) \propto p(\mathbf{t}|l, \mathcal{R}) \tag{3.11}$$

where the tracklet index i and the dependency on the parameters Θ have been dropped for clarity of notation. In order to keep inference tractable, we marginalize over l when estimating the road model parameters $\mathcal{R}$. When estimating the location of individual objects in the scene, the posterior over l becomes important and is explicitly computed. The tracklet distribution conditioned on the lane and road layout is given by

$$p(\mathbf{t}|l, \mathcal{R}) = \begin{cases} p_l(\mathbf{t}|l, \mathcal{R}) & \text{if } l \leq K(K-1) \quad \text{(lane)} \\ p_p(\mathbf{t}|l, \mathcal{R}) & \text{if } K(K-1) < l \leq 2K \quad \text{(parking)} \end{cases}$$

$$(3.12)$$

where $p_l(\mathbf{t}|l, \mathcal{R})$ and $p_p(\mathbf{t}|l, \mathcal{R})$ denote the likelihood terms for the lanes and parking areas, respectively.

In order to evaluate the tracklet posterior for lanes $p_l(\mathbf{t}|l, \mathcal{R})$, all object detections $\mathbf{t} = \{\mathbf{d}_1, \ldots, \mathbf{d}_{M_d}\}$ must be associated to locations on the spline of lane l. As this subroutine is called very often during inference (i.e., once per sample and observed tracklet) and for maintaining efficiency, we discretize the lane spline at 1m intervals and augment the observation model with an additional discrete latent variable s per object detection $\mathbf{d}$ which indexes the location on the lane as illustrated in Fig. 3.2(a). Note that a 1m discretization interval is sufficient as for most viewpoints the observation noise will be larger than 1m. As dynamical model we employ a left-to-right Hidden Markov Model. Marginalizing over all hidden states $\{s_1, \ldots, s_{M_d}\}$ yields

$$\begin{aligned} p_l(\mathbf{t}|l, \mathcal{R}) &= \sum_{s_1, \ldots, s_{M_d}} p_l(\mathbf{t}, s_1, \ldots, s_{M_d}|l, \mathcal{R}) \\ &= \sum_{s_1, \ldots, s_{M_d}} p(s_1) p_l(\mathbf{d}_1|s_1, l, \mathcal{R}) \\ &\quad \times \prod_{j=2}^{M_d} p(s_j|s_{j-1}) p_l(\mathbf{d}_j|s_j, l, \mathcal{R}) \end{aligned}$$

$$(3.13)$$

where M_d denotes the number of object detections in the tracklet and tracklets are allowed to start anywhere on the lane with equal probability, i.e., $s_1 \sim \mathcal{U}(\{1, \ldots, M_l\})$, with M_l the number of spline points on lane l. Our motion model is simple, yet effective: By constraining all tracklets to move forward with uniform probability

$$p(s_j|s_{j-1}) = \begin{cases} \frac{1}{M_l - s_{j-1} + 1} & \text{if } s_j \geq s_{j-1} \\ 0 & \text{otherwise} \end{cases} \qquad (3.14)$$

the model is able to distinguish the lane of a crossing street purely based on the vehicle's motion. This is of importance as distance measurements of far objects are noisy to an extend which is preventing the distinction from the object location alone. The emission probability for lanes $p_l(\mathbf{d}|s, l, \mathcal{R})$ is factorized into the probability over object location $\mathbf{m}_d, \mathbf{S}_d$ and object orientation $\mathbf{o}_d$

$$p_l(\mathbf{d}|s, l, \mathcal{R}) = p(\mathbf{m}_d|s, l, \mathcal{R}, \mathbf{S}_d)\, p(\mathbf{o}_d|s, l, \mathcal{R}) \qquad (3.15)$$

For clarity of notation the detection index j has been dropped. The 3D object location in Eq. 3.15 is modeled as a Gaussian mixture

$$\begin{aligned} p(\mathbf{m}_d|s, l, \mathcal{R}, \mathbf{S}_d) &= (1 - \zeta_t)\, p_{in}(\mathbf{m}_d|s, l, \mathcal{R}, \mathbf{S}_d) \\ &+ \zeta_t\, p_{out}(\mathbf{m}_d|s, l, \mathcal{R}) \end{aligned} \qquad (3.16)$$

with inlier and outlier distributions defined by

$$p_{in}(\mathbf{m}_d|s, l, \mathcal{R}, \mathbf{S}_d) \propto \exp\left(-\frac{1}{2}(\phi_t - \mathbf{m}_d)^\mathsf{T}\mathbf{S}_d^{-1}(\phi_t - \mathbf{m}_d)\right)$$

$$p_{out}(\mathbf{m}_d|s, l, \mathcal{R}) \propto \exp\left(-\frac{1}{2\sigma_{out}^2}\mathbf{m}_d^\mathsf{T}\mathbf{m}_d\right), \qquad (3.17)$$

respectively. Here, $\phi_t(s, l, \mathcal{R}) \in \mathbb{R}^2$ denotes the 2D location of spline point s on lane l according to the B-spline model presented in Section 3.1, $\zeta_t \in \Theta$ is the outlier probability and $\sigma_{out} \in \Theta$ is a parameter controlling the 'spread' of the outlier distribution.

For the object orientation likelihood, we impose a categorical distribution over object orientations $\mathbf{o}_d$

$$p(\mathbf{o}_d|s, l, \mathcal{R}) = \mathcal{C}at(\varphi_t(s, l, \mathcal{R})|\mathbf{o}_d) = o_{d, \varphi_t(s, l, \mathcal{R})} \qquad (3.18)$$

where $\varphi_t(s, l, \mathcal{R}) \in \{1, \ldots, 8\}$ selects the orientation bin that represents the relative direction the object would be viewed by the observer when it was driving into the direction of the lane. Intuitively, Eq. 3.18 encourages lane associations such that the estimated vehicle orientation and the direction of the lane coincide. The relative viewing direction is computed from the tangent of lane l at spline point s.

For parking areas, all cars are assumed to be static. Thus, no dynamics needs to be incorporated into the observation model and the tracklet's parking area likelihood reduces to

$$
\begin{aligned}
p_p(\mathbf{t}|l, \mathcal{R}) &= \sum_s p_p(\mathbf{t}, s|l, \mathcal{R}) \\
&= \sum_s \prod_{j=1}^{M_d} p(s)\, p_p(\mathbf{d}_j|s, l, \mathcal{R})
\end{aligned}
\tag{3.19}
$$

assuming a uniform prior $p(s)$ on the location s within parking area l. Furthermore, for parked cars we do not make any assumption about the orientation. Thus, the emission probability becomes

$$
p_p(\mathbf{d}|s, l, \mathcal{R}) = \frac{1}{8}\, p(\mathbf{m}_d|s, l, \mathcal{R}, \mathbf{S}_d)
\tag{3.20}
$$

with $p(\mathbf{m}_d|s, l, \mathcal{R}, \mathbf{S}_d)$ as in Eq. 3.16.

3.3.3. Vanishing Points

Assuming all $N_v \in \{0, 1, 2\}$ vanishing points $\mathcal{V} = \{v_1, \ldots, v_{N_v}\}$, represented by their orientations on the ground plane $v_i \in [0, \pi)$, to be independent given the road layout $\mathcal{R}$, we define

$$
p(v|\mathcal{R}, \Theta) \propto \zeta_v + (1 - \zeta_v) \exp\left(-\lambda_v \phi_v(v, \mathcal{R}, \Theta)\right)
\tag{3.21}
$$

with orientation error

$$\phi_v(v, \mathcal{R}, \Theta) = 1 - \cos(2v - 2\varphi_v(\mathcal{R})) \qquad (3.22)$$

where $\zeta_v \in \Theta$ is a small constant capturing outlier detections. The last term in Eq. 3.21 correspond to the cyclic von Mises distribution [22] up to a normalizing factor that depends on the zeroth-order Bessel function of the first kind. $\varphi_v(\mathcal{R})$ is the orientation of the closest street, based on the current road model configuration $\mathcal{R}$, and $\lambda_v \in \Theta$ is a precision parameter and controls the importance of this term. As lines belonging to a vanishing point are undirected, i.e., $v \in [0, \pi)$ instead of $v \in [0, 2\pi)$, a factor of 2 is added in Eq. 3.22 to accommodate this fact.

3.3.4. Semantic Scene Labels

Let $s \in \mathcal{S}$ represent the (discrete) distribution over the three different semantic classes 'road', 'background' and 'sky' for a particular image patch. The semantic label likelihood for that patch is modeled as

$$p(s|\mathcal{R}, \Theta) \propto \exp\left(\frac{\lambda_s}{N_s}\, w_{s,\phi_s(\mathcal{R})}\, s_{\phi_s(\mathcal{R})}\right) \qquad (3.23)$$

where $\lambda_s \in \Theta$ is a parameter controlling the importance of the semantic label cue, $\phi_s(\mathcal{R}) \in \{1, 2, 3\}$ picks the class label corresponding to the same pixel in a 'virtual' segmentation of the scene according to the current road model configuration $\mathcal{R}$ and $\mathbf{w}_s \in \mathbb{R}^3$ is a weight vector. We assume that the background (i.e., buildings, trees) starts directly behind the curb of the road and buildings reach a height of four stories on average, thereby defining the background area which separates the sky from the road region. Facades adjacent to the observer's own street are not considered. Despite the fact that this approximation seems quite crude, many inner-city scenes in our dataset follow this scheme closely. Fig. 3.4 illustrates the scene labeling returned by our boosting classifier described in Section 4.3 (left) as well as the labeling generated from the re-projection of our

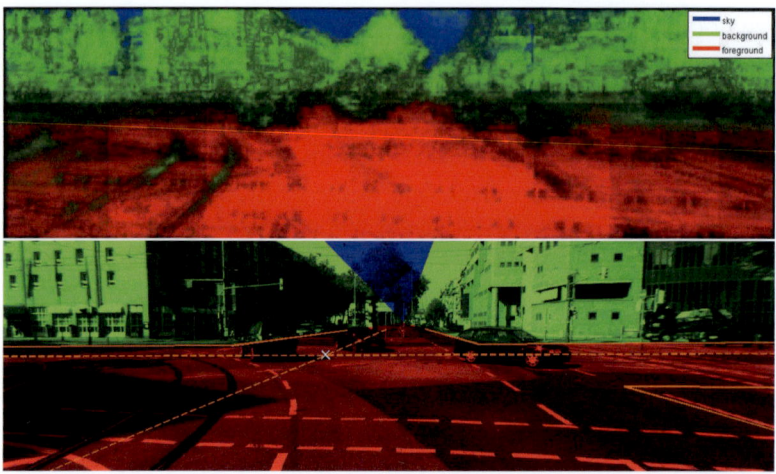

Figure 3.4.: **Illustration of Scene Label Likelihood.** This figure shows
the semantic segmentation returned by a joint boosting classifier (top) and
the 'virtual' image segmentation corresponding to the current road layout
configuration $\mathcal{R}$ (bottom). The semantic scene label likelihood in Eq. 3.23
encourages a large overlap between the virtual segmentation and the classification result.

model (right). A large overlap corresponds to a large likelihood in
Eq. 3.23.

3.3.5. Scene Flow

Compared to the tracklet observations, the 3D scene flow likelihood
directly explains all moving objects in the scene with the road model
described by $\mathcal{R}$. However, in contrast to vehicle tracklets, objects
that do not fit the appearance model of the car detector (e.g., trucks,
tractors, quad bikes, motorbikes) and hence have been missed at detection time are considered here as well, unless they do not move.

Recall that each 3D flow vector $\mathbf{f} = (\mathbf{p}_f, \mathbf{q}_f)$ is defined by its
location $\mathbf{p}_f$ and normalized velocity $\mathbf{q}_f$ on the road plane. The probability of a scene flow vector depends on its proximity to the closest

lane and on how well its velocity vector aligns with the tangent of the respective B-spline at the corresponding foot point

$$p(\mathbf{f}|\mathcal{R}, \Theta) \propto \phi_f(\mathbf{f}, \mathcal{R}, \Theta)^{\frac{1}{N_f}} \qquad (3.24)$$

where

$$\phi_f(\mathbf{f}, \mathcal{R}, \Theta) = \zeta_f \exp\left(-\frac{\|\mathbf{p}_f\|_2^2}{2\sigma_{out}^2}\right) + (1 - \zeta_f)\exp\left(-\tilde{\phi}_f(\mathbf{f}, \mathcal{R}, \Theta)\right) \qquad (3.25)$$

and

$$\tilde{\phi}_f(\mathbf{f}, \mathcal{R}, \Theta) = -\lambda_{f1}\|\mathbf{p}_f - \boldsymbol{\varphi}_f(\mathbf{p}_f, \mathcal{R})\|_2^2 - \lambda_{f2}(1 - \mathbf{q}_f^\mathsf{T}\tilde{\boldsymbol{\varphi}}_f(\mathbf{p}_f, \mathcal{R})) \qquad (3.26)$$

with parameters $\zeta_f, \lambda_{f1}, \lambda_{f2}, \sigma_{out} \in \Theta$. Here, ζ_f accounts for outliers and λ_{f1} and λ_{f2} control the importance of the location and the orientation term, respectively. Similar to the vehicle tracklet model from Section 3.3.2, σ_{out} denotes the width of the outlier distribution. The functions $\boldsymbol{\varphi}_f(\mathbf{p}_f, \mathcal{R}) \in \mathbb{R}^2$ and $\tilde{\boldsymbol{\varphi}}_f(\mathbf{p}_f, \mathcal{R}) \in \mathbb{R}^2$ return the spline foot point and tangent vector at the location closest to $\mathbf{p}_f$, respectively. This is illustrated in Fig. 3.5(a). The dependencies are modeled as a hard mixture, i.e. for each flow vector we select the spline l that maximizes Eq. 3.24.

3.3.6. Occupancy Grid

Free space information is incorporated by means of a 2D occupancy grid $\mathcal{O} = \{\rho_1, \ldots, \rho_{N_o}\}$, modeled in road coordinates ($y = 0$), with N_o the number of cells in the grid. Here, our assumption is that the road area should coincide with free space while non-road areas may be covered by buildings or vegetation. Each cell ρ in the grid takes one of three values $\rho \in \{-1, 0, +1\}$ representing free space, unobserved areas and obstacles. The occupancy likelihood of cell ρ

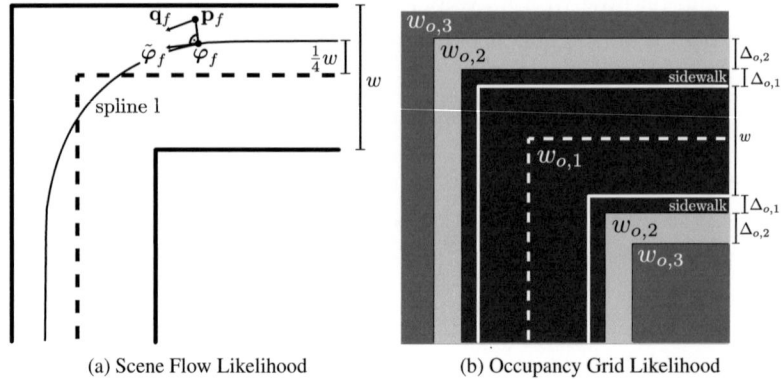

(a) Scene Flow Likelihood   (b) Occupancy Grid Likelihood

Figure 3.5.: **Scene Flow and Occupancy Grid Observation Model.** (a) The proposed scene flow likelihood encourages flow vectors to agree with the lane geometry. (b) The geometric prior, a 'template' of freespace and occupied areas, determines the occupancy grid likelihood.

is defined as

$$p(\rho|\mathcal{R}, \Theta) \propto \exp\left(\frac{\lambda_o}{N_o} \rho \cdot \phi_o(\mathcal{R})\right) \tag{3.27}$$

where $\phi_o(\mathcal{R}) \in \{w_{o,1}, w_{o,2}, w_{o,3}\}$ is a mapping that for any cell ρ returns the value (or weight) of a model-dependent geometric prior expressing the belief on the location of free space (i.e., road) and buildings alongside the road. The geometric prior is illustrated in Fig. 3.5(b) for the case of a right turn. Intuitively, it encourages free space where the road is located and obstacles elsewhere, with a preference towards the roadside region. $\lambda_o \in \Theta$ controls the strength of this term.

3.4. Inference

Given the image evidence $\mathcal{E}$, we are interested in determining the underlying road layout $\mathcal{R}$ and the location of cars $\mathcal{C} = \{(l, s)\}$ in the scene

$$\hat{\mathcal{R}}, \hat{\mathcal{C}} = \underset{\mathcal{R},\mathcal{C}}{\operatorname{argmax}} \; p(\mathcal{R}, \mathcal{C} | \mathcal{E}, \Theta) \tag{3.28}$$

where l denotes the lane index and s contains the spline points of all detections in a tracklet. Unfortunately, the posteriors involved in this computation have no analytical solution and can't be solved in closed form. Thus we approximate them using Metropolis-Hastings sampling [5, 78, 86, 123, 79]. A short review on the sampling techniques employed in this thesis is given in Appendix A. To keep computations tractable, the problem is split into two sub-problems: First, we estimate $\mathcal{R}$ while marginalizing $\mathcal{C}$

$$\hat{\mathcal{R}} = \underset{\mathcal{R}}{\operatorname{argmax}} \; p(\mathcal{R} | \mathcal{E}, \Theta) = \underset{\mathcal{R}}{\operatorname{argmax}} \sum_{\mathcal{C}} p(\mathcal{R}, \mathcal{C} | \mathcal{E}, \Theta) \tag{3.29}$$

Given an estimate of $\mathcal{R}$, the object locations $\mathcal{C}$ can be inferred as

$$\hat{\mathcal{C}} = \underset{\mathcal{C}}{\operatorname{argmax}} \; p(\mathcal{C} | \mathcal{E}, \mathcal{R}, \Theta) \tag{3.30}$$

Both steps are detailed in the following two subsections. Throughout inference, the calibration parameters, the camera poses and the ground plane are assumed to be known, i.e., estimated with sufficient accuracy, and fixed.

3.4.1. Inferring the Road Layout

Our first goal is to estimate the road layout $\mathcal{R}$ given the image evidence $\mathcal{E}$

$$\hat{\mathcal{R}} = \underset{\mathcal{R}}{\operatorname{argmax}} \, p(\mathcal{R} | \mathcal{E}, \Theta) \tag{3.31}$$

where

$$p(\mathcal{R} | \mathcal{E}, \Theta) \propto p(\mathcal{E}, \mathcal{R} | \Theta) \tag{3.32}$$

as $p(\mathcal{E})$ is constant. For computing the maximum a-posteriori estimate in Eq. 3.31 we run a Markov chain for n_{infer} iterations and

Local Metropolis Proposals (33%)
1. Vary center of crossroads $\mathbf{c}$ ($\sigma_{\mathbf{c}}$)
2. Vary width of all roads $\mathbf{w}$ ($\sigma_{\mathbf{w}}$)
3. Vary angle of crossing street α (σ_{α})
4. Vary overall orientation r (σ_r)
5. Vary center $\mathbf{c}$ and width $\mathbf{w}$ jointly
6. Vary center $\mathbf{c}$, width $\mathbf{w}$, angle α and rotation r jointly
Inter-Topology Metropolis Proposals (33%)
7. Re-sample κ uniformly
Global Metropolis-Hastings Proposals (33%)
8. Re-sample all parameters $\mathcal{R} = \{\kappa, \mathbf{c}, w, r, \alpha\}$ from the prior

Table 3.1.: **Metropolis-Hastings Proposals for Inference.** We randomly propose one of the above moves with probability given in brackets and accept the move according to the acceptance probability in Eq. 3.33.

pick the sample with the highest probability. As the normalization constant $p(\mathcal{E})$ does not depend on $\mathcal{R}$, it cancels in the sampler's acceptance ratio

$$
\begin{aligned}
p_{MH}(\mathcal{R}'|\mathcal{R}) &= \min\left\{1, \frac{p(\mathcal{R}'|\mathcal{E}, \Theta)q(\mathcal{R}|\mathcal{R}', \Theta)}{p(\mathcal{R}|\mathcal{E}, \Theta)q(\mathcal{R}'|\mathcal{R}, \Theta)}\right\} \\
&= \min\left\{1, \frac{p(\mathcal{E}, \mathcal{R}'|\Theta)q(\mathcal{R}|\mathcal{R}', \Theta)}{p(\mathcal{E}, \mathcal{R}|\Theta)q(\mathcal{R}'|\mathcal{R}, \Theta)}\right\}
\end{aligned} \quad (3.33)
$$

Here, $q(\mathcal{R}'|\mathcal{R}, \Theta)$ denotes the proposal distribution and $\mathcal{R}'$ is the proposed state computed from the old state $\mathcal{R}$ using one of the moves in Table 3.1. A short tutorial on sampling techniques and Metropolis-Hastings can be found in Appendix A.

We exploit a combination of *local, inter-topology* and *global* moves to obtain a well-mixing Markov chain. While local moves modify $\mathcal{R}$ slightly, global moves sample $\mathcal{R}$ directly from the prior. This ensures a quick traversal of the search space, while still exploring local modes. For local moves we choose symmetric proposals

---

Algorithm 1 Tracklet Marginals (Forward Algorithm)

Input: $\mathbf{E} = [\mathbf{e}_1, \ldots, \mathbf{e}_{M_d}]$, $E_{j,s} \propto p_l(\mathbf{d}_j|s, l, \mathcal{R})$

Output: $\log p_l(\mathbf{t}|l, \mathcal{R})$

$\boldsymbol{\alpha}_1 \leftarrow \frac{1}{M_s}\mathbf{e}_1$

$\beta \leftarrow \sum_{k=1}^{M_s} \alpha_{1,k}$, $\boldsymbol{\alpha}_1 \leftarrow \frac{1}{\beta}\boldsymbol{\alpha}_1$, $\log p_l \leftarrow \log \beta$

for $j \leftarrow 2, \ldots, M_d$ **do**

    for $k \leftarrow 1, \ldots, M_s$ **do**

        $\alpha_{j,k} \leftarrow E_{j,k} \frac{1}{k} \sum_{k'=1}^{k} \alpha_{j-1,k'}$

    $\beta \leftarrow \sum_k \alpha_{j,k}$, $\boldsymbol{\alpha}_j \leftarrow \frac{1}{\beta}\boldsymbol{\alpha}_j$, $\log p_l \leftarrow \log p_l + \log \beta$

return $\log p_l$

---

in the form of Gaussians centered on the previous state such that the proposal ratio in Eq. 3.33 cancels. To avoid trans-dimensional jumps [82], we do not alter the existence of the variable α. Instead, we include α in all models, also when $\kappa = 1$. Table 3.1 gives an overview of the move categories picked at random. Note that while the local and inter-topology moves are symmetric and thus purely 'Metropolis', the global moves result in a proposal distribution ratio $q(\mathcal{R}|\mathcal{R}', \Theta)/q(\mathcal{R}'|\mathcal{R}, \Theta) \neq 1$.

Each sample requires the evaluation of $p(\mathcal{R}|\mathcal{E}, \Theta)$ up to a normalizing constant. The marginalization in Eq. 3.13 can be carried out efficiently using the forward algorithm [22] for hidden Markov models, which for the dynamical model in Eq. 3.14 is given in Algorithm 1. Numerical instabilities due to limitations in the floating point arithmetic precision are mitigated through proper re-normalization in each step of the algorithm.

3.4.2. Inferring the Location of Objects

Given the road model $\mathcal{R}$, we are interested in recovering the location of cars $\mathcal{C} = \{(l_1, \mathbf{s}_1), \ldots, (l_{N_t}, \mathbf{s}_{N_t})\}$, where l_i denotes the lane index and $\mathbf{s}_i$ are the spline indices of all detections in tracklet i

$$\hat{C} = \underset{C}{\operatorname{argmax}} \ p(C|\mathcal{E}, \mathcal{R}, \Theta) \qquad (3.34)$$

Conditioned on $\mathcal{R}$, all tracklets become independent such that the inference problem decomposes into sub-problems. Neglecting the tracklet index i and the dependency on Θ for notational clarity and observing that $p(\mathbf{t})$ is constant, l can be inferred by marginalizing over the object locations $\{s_1, \ldots, s_{M_d}\}$ on the lane spline

$$\hat{l} = \underset{l}{\operatorname{argmax}} \, p(l|\mathbf{t}, \mathcal{R}) = \underset{l}{\operatorname{argmax}} \, p(\mathbf{t}, l|\mathcal{R}) \qquad (3.35)$$

with $p(\mathbf{t}, l|\mathcal{R})$ defined by Eq. 3.11. Given l, the object locations on the lane spline

$$
\begin{aligned}
\hat{s}_1, \ldots, \hat{s}_{M_d} &= \underset{s_1, \ldots, s_{M_d}}{\operatorname{argmax}} \, p_l(s_1, \ldots, s_{M_d}|\mathbf{t}, l, \mathcal{R}) \\
&= \underset{s_1, \ldots, s_{M_d}}{\operatorname{argmax}} \, p_l(\mathbf{t}, s_1, \ldots, s_{M_d}|l, \mathcal{R}) \qquad (3.36)
\end{aligned}
$$

are easily inferred using Viterbi decoding for hidden Markov models. The procedure is sketched in Algorithm 2, assuming uniform forward motion probability as discussed in Section 3.3.2.

3.5. Learning

A principled way to estimate the parameters Θ of our model is to learn them from training data using maximum likelihood. Let us assume we are given a training set $(\mathcal{E}, \mathcal{R})$ of cardinality D, with $\mathcal{E} = \{\mathcal{E}_1, \ldots, \mathcal{E}_D\}$ denoting the image evidence and $\mathcal{R} = \{\mathcal{R}_1, \ldots, \mathcal{R}_D\}$ the annotated road layouts for each sequence, respectively. We perform ten-fold cross-validation. As we have 113 annotated sequences in total this leads to $D \approx 113 - 11 = 102$ training sequences per fold. For the ease of indexing, let us further assume that all model parameters are absorbed into the parameter set $\Theta = \{\theta_1, \ldots, \theta_{M_\Theta}\}$,

---

Algorithm 2 Vehicle Locations (Viterbi Decoding)

Input: $\mathbf{E} = [\mathbf{e}_1, \ldots, \mathbf{e}_{M_d}]$, $E_{j,s} \propto p_l(\mathbf{d}_j | s, l, \mathcal{R})$

Output: $\{s_1, \ldots, s_{M_d}\} = \mathrm{argmax}_{s_1,\ldots,s_{M_d}} \, p_l(s_1, \ldots, s_{M_d} | \mathbf{t}, l, \mathcal{R})$

$\delta_1 \leftarrow \frac{1}{M_s} \mathbf{e}_1$

for $j \leftarrow 2, \ldots, M_d$ **do**

    for $k \leftarrow 1, \ldots, M_s$ **do**

        $\delta_{j,k} \leftarrow E_{j,k} \, \max_{k'=1,\ldots,k} \delta_{j-1,k'}$

        $\psi_{j,k} \leftarrow \mathrm{argmax}_{k'=1,\ldots,k} \delta_{j-1,k'}$

$s_{M_d} \leftarrow \psi_{M_d, M_s}$

for $j \leftarrow M_d - 1, \ldots, 1$ **do**

    $s_j \leftarrow \psi_{j+1, s_{j+1}}$

return $\{s_1, \ldots, s_{M_d}\}$

---

with θ_i denoting a single parameter (e.g., λ_t, λ_v, ...) and M_Θ is the total number of parameters.

3.5.1. Learning the Model Parameters

Given a training fold $(\mathcal{E}, \mathcal{R})$, our goal is to find the parameter set $\hat{\Theta}$ that maximizes the likelihood of the data

$$\hat{\Theta} = \mathrm{argmax}_{\Theta} \, p(\mathcal{E}, \mathcal{R} | \Theta) \tag{3.37}$$

with

$$p(\mathcal{E}, \mathcal{R} | \Theta) = \prod_{d=1}^{D} p(\mathcal{E}_d, \mathcal{R}_d | \Theta) \tag{3.38}$$

Unfortunately, maximizing Eq. 3.38 directly for Θ is intractable due to the integral over $\mathcal{R}$ that appears in the partition function

$$Z(\Theta) = \int p(\mathcal{E}, \mathcal{R} | \Theta) d\mathcal{R} \tag{3.39}$$

Instead, let us define a Gibbs random field by writing $p(\mathcal{E}_d, \mathcal{R}_d|\Theta)$ as

$$p(\mathcal{E}_d, \mathcal{R}_d|\Theta) = \frac{1}{Z_d(\Theta)} \exp\left(-\Psi(\mathcal{E}_d, \mathcal{R}_d, \Theta)\right) \tag{3.40}$$

where $\Psi(\mathcal{E}_d, \mathcal{R}_d, \Theta)$ is the sum of a set of potential functions $\{\psi_i\}$. Details on the shape of the individual potentials, corresponding to the prior and the likelihoods from Section 3.3 will be given in Section 3.5.2 and the resulting factor graph is depicted in Fig. 3.6. $Z_d(\Theta)$ is the partition function corresponding to data point d

$$Z_d(\Theta) = \int \exp(-\Psi(\mathcal{E}_d, \mathcal{R}, \Theta))d\mathcal{R} \tag{3.41}$$

necessary for turning $p(\mathcal{E}_d, \mathcal{R}_d|\Theta)$ into a proper distribution. Note that in Eq. 3.41 and in the following we abuse the integral over $\mathcal{R}$ to express integration *and* summation in order to avoid clutter in the notation. Substituting Eq. 3.40 into Eq. 3.38, we obtain

$$p(\mathcal{E}, \mathcal{R}|\Theta) = \frac{1}{Z(\Theta)} \exp\left(-\Psi(\mathcal{E}, \mathcal{R}, \Theta)\right) \tag{3.42}$$

with

$$\Psi(\mathcal{E}, \mathcal{R}, \Theta) = \sum_{d=1}^{D} \Psi(\mathcal{E}_d, \mathcal{R}_d, \Theta) \tag{3.43}$$

$$\text{and} \quad Z(\Theta) = \prod_{d=1}^{D} Z_d(\Theta) \tag{3.44}$$

The partition functions in Eq. 3.41 and Eq. 3.44, required for evaluating Eq. 3.38, are still intractable to compute. However, it is possible to approximate the gradients of the log-likelihood function

$$\mathcal{L}(\mathcal{E}, \mathcal{R}, \Theta) = \sum_{d=1}^{D} \log p(\mathcal{E}_d, \mathcal{R}_d | \Theta)$$

$$= -\sum_{d=1}^{D} (\Psi(\mathcal{E}_d, \mathcal{R}_d | \Theta) + \log Z_d(\Theta)) \quad (3.45)$$

which can be optimized as surrogate for Eq. 3.38. Taking the partial derivative of $\mathcal{L}(\mathcal{E}, \mathcal{R}, \Theta)$ with respect to parameter θ_i, we obtain

$$\frac{\partial}{\partial \theta_i} \mathcal{L}(\mathcal{E}, \mathcal{R}, \Theta) = -\sum_{d=1}^{D} \left(\frac{\partial}{\partial \theta_i} \Psi(\mathcal{E}_d, \mathcal{R}_d, \Theta) + \frac{\partial}{\partial \theta_i} \log Z_d(\Theta) \right)$$

$$(3.46)$$

While the first term in this sum can be evaluated easily as it only depends on the potential functions themselves, the second term seems intractable at first glance as it involves derivatives of the log-partition function. By re-arranging the terms, however, we obtain

$$\frac{\partial}{\partial \theta_i} \log Z_d(\Theta)$$

$$= \frac{1}{Z_d(\Theta)} \frac{\partial}{\partial \theta_i} Z_d(\Theta)$$

$$= \frac{1}{Z_d(\Theta)} \int \frac{\partial}{\partial \theta_i} \exp(-\Psi(\mathcal{E}_d, \mathcal{R}, \Theta)) d\mathcal{R}$$

$$= -\frac{1}{Z_d(\Theta)} \int \exp(-\Psi(\mathcal{E}_d, \mathcal{R}, \Theta)) \frac{\partial}{\partial \theta_i} \Psi(\mathcal{E}_d, \mathcal{R}, \Theta) d\mathcal{R}$$

$$= -\int p(\mathcal{E}_d, \mathcal{R} | \Theta) \frac{\partial}{\partial \theta_i} \Psi(\mathcal{E}_d, \mathcal{R}, \Theta) d\mathcal{R}$$

$$= -\left\langle \frac{\partial}{\partial \theta_i} \Psi(\mathcal{E}_d, \mathcal{R}, \Theta) \right\rangle_{p(\mathcal{E}_d, \mathcal{R} | \Theta)} \quad (3.47)$$

Here, the derivative with respect to θ_i and the integral operator can be swapped because the partial derivative of the integrand is continuous and the limits of integration do not depend on θ_i (Leibniz integral rule). Thus, the derivative of the log-partition function can be expressed as the expectation of the potential derivatives with respect to the model distribution $p(\mathcal{E}_d, \mathcal{R}|\Theta)$. In contrast to [92, 156] the potentials Ψ additionally depend on $\mathcal{E}_d$ in our case. While it is impossible to evaluate this expression exactly, it can be approximated by drawing samples using Markov Chain Monte Carlo as described in Section 3.4. Sampling exhaustively from the model distribution is computationally prohibitive. However, it has been shown [92] that when starting from the data distribution, a couple of sampling iterations, say n_{learn} iterations, are sufficient to draw the samples closer to the (current) model distribution. This change is sufficient to approximate the gradients well enough. Given the approximation to the gradient, we take n_{iter} steps into its direction

$$\delta\theta_i = -\frac{\eta_i}{D} \sum_{d=1}^{D} \left(\frac{\partial}{\partial\theta_i}\Psi(\mathcal{E}_d, \mathcal{R}_d, \Theta) + \left\langle \frac{\partial}{\partial\theta_i}\Psi(\mathcal{E}_d, \mathcal{R}, \Theta) \right\rangle_{p(\mathcal{E}_d, \mathcal{R}|\Theta)} \right) \tag{3.48}$$

where η_i is the learning rate controlling the speed of convergence. The choice of η_i is subtle: When η_i is chosen too small, the parameters converge very slowly. On contrary, values that are too large can easily cause parameter divergence. Furthermore, choosing a single η for all parameter dimensions i will inherently lead to slow convergence rates as η has to be chosen small enough such that convergence for all parameters is guaranteed.

Thus, we employ a simple optimization heuristic: We initialize all η_i small enough ($\eta_i = 10^{-6}$) and analyze the normalized second derivative of each parameter, which is an indicator for the smoothness of the learning curves, in a time interval of 10 iterations. For all smooth curves we multiply η_i by a factor of 10 while we divide all η_i's by 10 in case the curves become noisy. In practice, this algorithm led to quick and stable convergence. We also observed the procedure to be largely independent of the initialization, which has been empirically chosen for all parameters.

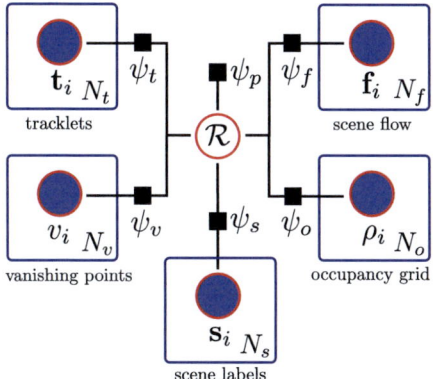

Figure 3.6.: **Factor Graph.** This figure shows the factor graph representation of the directed graphical model in Fig. 3.3 corresponding to the distribution in Eq. 3.49. Dependencies between random variables are expressed using factor nodes (black squares) and the latent tracklet variables s and l have been marginalized for clarity of presentation.

3.5.2. Energy Potentials and Derivatives

For applying the learning procedure described in Section 3.5.1, all potential functions[1] need to be properly defined and their derivatives with respect to the model parameters Θ must be calculated. The joint potential $\Psi(\mathcal{E}, \mathcal{R}, \Theta)$ from Eq. 3.40 decomposes as

$$\begin{aligned}
\Psi(\mathcal{E}, \mathcal{R}, \Theta) = {} & \psi_p(\mathcal{R}, \Theta) + \psi_t(\mathcal{T}, \mathcal{R}, \Theta) \\
& + \psi_v(\mathcal{V}, \mathcal{R}, \Theta) + \psi_s(\mathcal{S}, \mathcal{R}, \Theta) \\
& + \psi_f(\mathcal{F}, \mathcal{R}, \Theta) + \psi_o(\mathcal{O}, \mathcal{R}, \Theta)
\end{aligned} \tag{3.49}$$

using the same subscript notation as in Eq. 3.3. The corresponding factor graph is illustrated in Fig. 3.6. In the following, we derive each potential in Eq. 3.49.

---

[1]Note that throughout this section we call '$\psi(\cdot)$' a potential function for clarity of notation, even though (strictly speaking) '$-\psi(\cdot)$' is the actual energy potential.

Prior: By taking the negative logarithm of Eq. 3.4 and absorbing all constant terms into the partition function, we obtain the prior potential

$$\psi_p(\mathcal{R}, \Theta) = -\log \xi_{p,\kappa} - \lambda_p \log f_\kappa(\alpha)$$
$$+ \frac{1}{2} \phi_p(\mathcal{R}, \boldsymbol{\mu}_p^{(\kappa)})^\mathsf{T} \boldsymbol{\Lambda}_p^{(\kappa)} \phi_p(\mathcal{R}, \boldsymbol{\mu}_p^{(\kappa)}) \quad (3.50)$$

with

$$\phi_p(\mathcal{R}, \boldsymbol{\mu}_p^{(\kappa)}) = (\mathbf{c}, r, \log w)^\mathsf{T} - \boldsymbol{\mu}_p^{(\kappa)} \quad (3.51)$$

and $\boldsymbol{\xi}_p, \lambda_p \in \Theta$. While $\boldsymbol{\mu}_p \in \mathbb{R}^4$ can be parameterized element-wise, i.e. $\boldsymbol{\mu}_p \in \Theta$, $\boldsymbol{\Lambda}_p \in \mathbb{R}^{4\times4}$ has to fulfill the properties of a precision matrix, i.e. it must be symmetric positive definite. These properties can be enforced by considering the Cholesky decomposition of $\boldsymbol{\Lambda}$,

$$\boldsymbol{\Lambda} = \mathbf{L}^\mathsf{T}\mathbf{L} \quad (3.52)$$

into a lower triangular matrix $\mathbf{L}^\mathsf{T}$ and an upper triangular matrix $\mathbf{L}$, omitting all indices for clarity of notation. Clearly, $\boldsymbol{\Lambda}$ is symmetric positive definite and $\mathbf{L}$ can be parameterized as

$$\mathbf{L} = \begin{bmatrix} L_{1,1} & L_{1,2} & L_{1,3} & L_{1,4} \\ 0 & L_{2,2} & L_{2,3} & L_{2,4} \\ 0 & 0 & L_{3,3} & L_{3,4} \\ 0 & 0 & 0 & L_{4,4} \end{bmatrix} \quad (3.53)$$

with $\forall_{i \leq j}: L_{i,j} \in \Theta$. The required derivatives with respect to $\xi_{p,i}$, μ, $\mathbf{L}_{i,j}$ and λ_p are readily given by

$$\frac{\partial \psi_p(\mathcal{R}, \Theta)}{\partial \xi_{p,i}} = -\frac{[\kappa = i]}{\xi_{p,i}}$$

$$\frac{\partial \psi_p(\mathcal{R}, \Theta)}{\partial \mu} = -\mathbf{\Lambda} \, \phi_p(\mathcal{R}, \mu)$$

$$\frac{\partial \psi_p(\mathcal{R}, \Theta)}{\partial L_{i,j}} = \frac{1}{2} \phi_p(\mathcal{R}, \mu)^\mathsf{T} \left(\frac{\partial \mathbf{L}^\mathsf{T}}{\partial L_{i,j}} \mathbf{L} + \mathbf{L}^\mathsf{T} \frac{\partial \mathbf{L}}{\partial L_{i,j}} \right) \phi_p(\mathcal{R}, \mu)$$

$$\frac{\partial \psi_p(\mathcal{R}, \Theta)}{\partial \lambda_p} = -\log f_\kappa(\alpha) \tag{3.54}$$

In practice, one can directly optimize for $\log \xi_{p,i}$ instead of $\xi_{p,i}$ for stability.

Vehicle Tracklets: The potential corresponding to the vehicle tracklet likelihood and its derivative are obtained by taking the logarithm of Eq. 3.10 and differentiating it:

$$\psi_t(\mathcal{T}, \mathcal{R}, \Theta) = -\frac{\lambda_t}{N_t} \sum_{i=1}^{N_t} \log \left(\sum_{l=1}^{L} p(\mathbf{t}_i, l | \mathcal{R}) \right) \tag{3.55}$$

$$\frac{\partial \psi_t(\mathcal{T}, \mathcal{R}, \Theta)}{\partial \lambda_t} = -\frac{1}{N_t} \sum_{i=1}^{N_t} \log \left(\sum_{l=1}^{L} p(\mathbf{t}_i, l | \mathcal{R}) \right) \tag{3.56}$$

Here, $\lambda_t \in \Theta$ is a parameter controlling the strength of the feature cue and the tracklet probability $p(\mathbf{t}, l | \mathcal{R})$ is defined by Eq. 3.10. We have added an additional degree of freedom λ_t to the tracklet potential ψ_t, which accommodates for violations of the naïve Bayesian observation model and controls the relative strength of the tracklet feature with respect to the prior and all other features.

Vanishing Points: Similarly, the vanishing point potential and its derivative are obtained from Eq. 3.21 as

$$\psi_v(\cdot) = -\sum_{i=1}^{N_v} \log\left(\zeta_v + (1-\zeta_v)\exp\left(-\lambda_v\phi_v(v_i, \mathcal{R}, \Theta)\right)\right)$$

$$\frac{\partial\psi_v(\cdot)}{\partial\zeta_v} = -\sum_{i=1}^{N_v} \frac{1-\exp\left(-\lambda_v\phi_v(v_i, \mathcal{R}, \Theta)\right)}{\zeta_v + (1-\zeta_v)\exp\left(-\lambda_v\phi_v(v_i, \mathcal{R}, \Theta)\right)}$$

$$\frac{\partial\psi_v(\cdot)}{\partial\lambda_v} = -\sum_{i=1}^{N_v} \frac{(\zeta_v - 1)\exp\left(-\lambda_v\phi_v(v_i, \mathcal{R}, \Theta)\right)\phi_v(v_i, \mathcal{R}, \Theta)}{\zeta_v + (1-\zeta_v)\exp\left(-\lambda_v\phi_v(v_i, \mathcal{R}, \Theta)\right)}$$

$$(3.57)$$

with $\phi_v(v, \mathcal{R}, \Theta)$ measuring the error with respect to the orientation of the closest street as defined in Eq. 3.22.

Semantic Scene Labels: The semantic scene label potential is given by taking the logarithm of Eq. 3.23 and differentiating with respect to λ_s

$$\psi_s(\mathcal{S}, \mathcal{R}, \Theta) = -\frac{\lambda_s}{N_s}\sum_{i=1}^{N_s} w_{s,\phi_s(\mathcal{R})}\, s_{i,\phi_s(\mathcal{R})} \qquad (3.58)$$

$$\frac{\partial\psi_s(\mathcal{S}, \mathcal{R}, \Theta)}{\partial\lambda_s} = -\frac{1}{N_s}\sum_{i=1}^{N_s} w_{s,\phi_s(\mathcal{R})}\, s_{i,\phi_s(\mathcal{R})} \qquad (3.59)$$

where $\phi_s(\mathcal{R}) \in \{1, 2, 3\}$ selects the class label according to the segmentation of the scene induced by the current road layout $\mathcal{R}$. For further details, we refer the reader to Section 3.3.4 and the illustration in Fig. 3.4.

Scene Flow: The scene flow potential is obtained by taking the logarithm of Eq. 3.24 and differentiating with respect to the outlier constant ζ_f and the importance weights λ_{f1} (location) and λ_{f2} (orientation):

$$\psi_f(\cdot) = -\frac{1}{N_f} \sum_{i=1}^{N_f} \log \phi_f(\mathbf{f}_i, \mathcal{R}, \Theta) \qquad (3.60)$$

$$\frac{\partial \psi_f(\cdot)}{\partial \zeta_f} = -\sum_{i=1}^{N_f} \frac{\exp\left(-\frac{\|\mathbf{P}_{f,i}\|_2^2}{2\sigma_{out}^2}\right) - \exp\left(-\tilde{\phi}_f(\mathbf{f}_i, \mathcal{R}, \Theta)\right)}{N_f \, \phi_f(\mathbf{f}_i, \mathcal{R}, \Theta)}$$

$$\frac{\partial \psi_f(\cdot)}{\partial \lambda_{f1}} = -\sum_{i=1}^{N_f} \frac{(\zeta_f - 1)\exp\left(-\tilde{\phi}_f(\mathbf{f}_i, \mathcal{R}, \Theta)\right)}{N_f \, \phi_f(\mathbf{f}_i, \mathcal{R}, \Theta)} \frac{\partial \tilde{\phi}_f(\mathbf{f}_i, \mathcal{R}, \Theta)}{\partial \lambda_{f1}}$$

$$\frac{\partial \psi_f(\cdot)}{\partial \lambda_{f1}} = -\sum_{i=1}^{N_f} \frac{(\zeta_f - 1)\exp\left(-\tilde{\phi}_f(\mathbf{f}_i, \mathcal{R}, \Theta)\right)}{N_f \, \phi_f(\mathbf{f}_i, \mathcal{R}, \Theta)} \frac{\partial \tilde{\phi}_f(\mathbf{f}_i, \mathcal{R}, \Theta)}{\partial \lambda_{f2}}$$

with the unnormalized probability of a single scene flow vector given by

$$\phi_f(\mathbf{f}, \mathcal{R}, \Theta) = \zeta_f \exp\left(-\frac{\|\mathbf{p}_f\|_2^2}{2\sigma_{out}^2}\right) + (1 - \zeta_f)\exp\left(-\tilde{\phi}_f(\mathbf{f}, \mathcal{R}, \Theta)\right) \qquad (3.61)$$

and

$$\tilde{\phi}_f(\mathbf{f}, \mathcal{R}, \Theta) = -\lambda_{f1}\|\mathbf{p}_f - \boldsymbol{\varphi}_f(\mathbf{p}_f, \mathcal{R})\|_2^2 - \lambda_{f2}(1 - \mathbf{q}_f^\mathsf{T}\tilde{\boldsymbol{\varphi}}_f(\mathbf{p}_f, \mathcal{R})) \qquad (3.62)$$

The partial derivatives with respect to λ are given by

$$\frac{\partial \tilde{\phi}_f(\mathbf{f}, \mathcal{R}, \Theta)}{\partial \lambda_{f1}} = -\|\mathbf{p}_f - \boldsymbol{\varphi}_f(\mathbf{p}_f, \mathcal{R})\|_2^2 \qquad (3.63)$$

$$\frac{\partial \tilde{\phi}_f(\mathbf{f}, \mathcal{R}, \Theta)}{\partial \lambda_{f2}} = \mathbf{q}_f^\mathsf{T}\tilde{\boldsymbol{\varphi}}_f(\mathbf{p}_f, \mathcal{R}) - 1 \qquad (3.64)$$

with $\varphi_f(\mathbf{p}_f, \mathcal{R})$ and $\tilde{\varphi}_f(\mathbf{p}_f, \mathcal{R})$ returning the foot point and tangent of the closest lane spline as in Eq. 3.26 and illustrated in Fig. 3.5(a).

Occupancy Grid: Taking the logarithm of Eq. 3.27 and its derivative, the occupancy grid potential reads

$$\psi_o(\mathcal{O}, \mathcal{R}, \Theta) \; = \; -\frac{\lambda_o}{N_o} \sum_{i=1}^{N_o} \rho_i \cdot \phi_o(\mathcal{R}) \qquad (3.65)$$

$$\frac{\partial \psi_o(\mathcal{O}, \mathcal{R}, \Theta)}{\partial \lambda_o} \; = \; -\frac{1}{N_o} \sum_{i=1}^{N_o} \rho_i \cdot \phi_o(\mathcal{R}) \qquad (3.66)$$

where $\phi_o(\mathcal{R}) \in \{w_{o,1}, w_{o,2}, w_{o,3}\}$ is a mapping that for any cell ρ returns the value of the model-dependent geometric prior expressing the belief on the location of free space (i.e. road) and buildings alongside the road. For more details the reader is referred to Section 3.27 and the illustration in Fig. 3.5(b).

4. Image Evidence

This chapter describes the feature cues used by our probabilistic model described in Section 3.3. They can be categorized into monocular cues (i.e., vehicle tracklets, vanishing points and semantic scene labels) for which one camera is sufficient and stereo cues (i.e., 3D scene flow and occupancy grids) which require a stereo camera setup. We represent all features in the reference coordinate system which as described in Chapter 3 is located below the left camera coordinate system in the last frame of each sequence as illustrated in Fig. 4.3. The required ego-motion falls off as a by-product when computing the scene flow features as described in Section 4.4.

4.1. Vehicle Tracklets

Vehicle tracklets are sets of vehicle detections which are associated over time and represent one of the strongest cues in our framework. This is because the observation of moving objects tells us a lot about the structure of the scene as well as where the lanes are located and which vehicles are allowed to move given the current traffic light situation. Empirically, we found that pedestrians occur much more rarely in our datasets and are thus less important in this context. While it would be straightforward to extend our model to include pedestrians, we focus on vehicles (i.e., cars) here. As we are interested in reasoning about the scene in bird's eye perspective, we also propose a way to extract 3D location estimates from the 2D object detections.

As mentioned earlier, we define a tracklet as a set of object detections, projected into bird's eye perspective $\mathbf{t} = \{\mathbf{d}_1, \ldots, \mathbf{d}_{M_d}\}$ with $\mathbf{d} = (f_d, \mathbf{m}_d, \mathbf{S}_d, \mathbf{o}_d)$. Here, $f_d \in \mathbb{N}$ is the frame number and

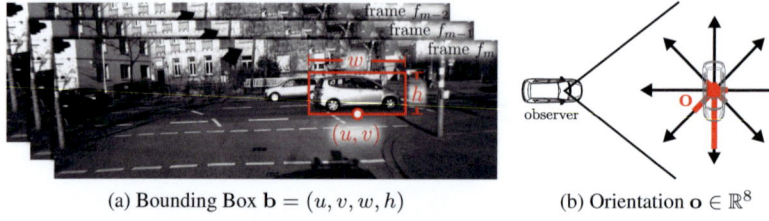

(a) Bounding Box $\mathbf{b} = (u, v, w, h)$ (b) Orientation $\mathbf{o} \in \mathbb{R}^8$

Figure 4.1.: **Illustration of Vehicle Detections.** We detect objects in adjacent frames, estimate their orientation and associate them over time.

$\mathbf{m}_d \in \mathbb{R}^2, \mathbf{S}_d \in \mathbb{R}^{2 \times 2}$ are the mean and covariance of the Gaussian distribution $\mathcal{N}(\mathbf{m}, \mathbf{S})$ describing the object location in road coordinates. $\mathbf{o}_d \in \Delta^7$ is a discrete orientation distribution over 8 possible points of view. The goal of the tracking stage is to associate object detections to tracklets and project them into 3D using cues such as the object size or the bounding box ground contact point in combination with the height and the pitch angle of the camera. Association of detections to tracklets is performed in image-scale space to better account for uncertainties of the object detector.

4.1.1. Detection

First, let us define a 2D object detection as $\tilde{\mathbf{d}} = (f, \mathbf{b}, \mathbf{o})^1$, with frame index $f \in \mathbb{N}$ and 2D object bounding box $\mathbf{b} = (u, v, w, h) \in \mathbb{R}^4$, where $(u, v)^\mathsf{T}$ is the bottom-center and $(w, h)^\mathsf{T}$ are the width and height of the bounding box. In contrast to most traditional object detectors, we also estimate a (discrete) distribution over 8 possible points of view, $\mathbf{o} \in \Delta^7$, giving us a sense of orientation of the object. All involved variables are illustrated in Fig. 4.1.

In order to detect objects $\{(f, \mathbf{b}, \mathbf{o})\}$ in an image, we train the part-based object detector[2] of [60] on a large set of manually annotated

---

[1] We use a tilde for distinguishing 2D object detections $\tilde{\mathbf{d}}$ (or vehicle tracklets $\tilde{\mathbf{t}}$) from 3D detections $\mathbf{d}$ (or vehicle tracklets $\mathbf{t}$)

[2] Source code available at: http://people.cs.uchicago.edu/~rbg/latent/

Algorithm 3 Multi-Class Non-Maximum-Suppression

Input: L-SVM detections with orientation and score $\{(\mathbf{b}, o, s)\}$
Output: NMS detections with orientation distribution $\{(\mathbf{b}, \mathbf{o})\}$
$\mathcal{A} \leftarrow \{(\mathbf{b}, o, s)\}$
$\mathcal{B} \leftarrow \emptyset$
while $\mathcal{A} \neq \emptyset$ **do**
    // Get all detections that overlap with the highest scoring one
    $\mathbf{a} \leftarrow \operatorname{argmax}_{\mathbf{x} \in \mathcal{A}} score(\mathbf{x})$
    $\mathcal{A}_{\mathbf{a}} \leftarrow \left\{ \mathbf{x} \mid \mathbf{x} \in \mathcal{A} \wedge \frac{box(\mathbf{x}) \cap box(\mathbf{a})}{box(\mathbf{x}) \cup box(\mathbf{a})} > \tau_d \right\}$
    // For each orientation, get highest score within $\mathcal{A}_{\mathbf{a}}$
    for $i \leftarrow 1, \ldots, 8$ **do**
        $\mathcal{A}_i \leftarrow \{\mathbf{x} \mid \mathbf{x} \in \mathcal{A}_{\mathbf{a}} \wedge orientation(\mathbf{x}) = i\}$
        $o_i \leftarrow \max_{\mathbf{x} \in \mathcal{A}_i} score(\mathbf{x})$
    // Apply softmax normalization
    $Z \leftarrow \sum_i \exp(o_i)$
    for $i \leftarrow 1, \ldots, 8$ **do**
        $o_i \leftarrow \frac{1}{Z} \exp(o_i)$
    // Add detection to $\mathcal{B}$ and remove $\mathcal{A}_{\mathbf{a}}$ from $\mathcal{A}$
    $\mathcal{B} \leftarrow \mathcal{B} \cup (box(\mathbf{a}), \mathbf{o})$
    $\mathcal{A} \leftarrow \mathcal{A} \setminus \mathcal{A}_{\mathbf{a}}$
return $\mathcal{B}$

---

images. The object detection system described in [60] is based on mixtures of multi-scale deformable part models, can represent highly variable object classes and achieves state-of-the-art performance in difficult scenarios such as the ones presented in the PASCAL object detection challenge [59]. For training object models we employ a latent SVM [60] where the location of the individual parts of an object are assumed to be unknown at training time and maximized over. The model parameters are found using stochastic gradient descent, embedded into an alternating scheme which also estimates the hidden variables at the same time.

In contrast to the original model of [60], our annotations do not

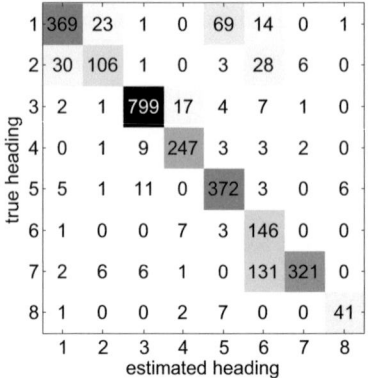
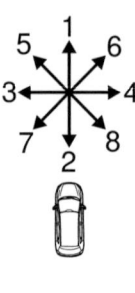

Figure 4.2.: **Confusion Matrix** of the orientation estimates by the part-based object detector presented in [60], trained in a semi-supervised fashion.

only comprise the bounding boxes **b**, but also the relative object orientations **o**, discretized into 8 viewpoints as illustrated in Fig. 4.1(b). We use one component per viewpoint and fix the latent variables such that they correspond to the components according to the ground truth orientations relative to the observer. By introducing this additional degree of supervision we are able to recover a distribution over possible object orientations $\mathbf{o} \in \Delta^7$ at test time for each detected object. Algorithm 3 illustrates the non-maximum-suppression mechanism which computes a small number of non-maximum suppressed detections with discrete orientation distributions from all raw detections with associated orientation and score. In order to obtain a proper distribution $\mathbf{o} \in \Delta^7$ with $\sum_i o_i = 1$, the softmax transformation is applied to the maximum of all detections scores over all orientation bins. Fig. 4.2 illustrates the quality of the MAP orientation estimate in terms of the confusion matrix over orientation classes.

4.1.2. Tracking

The association of 2D object detections $\{\tilde{\mathbf{d}}\}$ to 2D object tracks $\tilde{\mathbf{t}} = \{\tilde{\mathbf{d}}_1, \ldots, \tilde{\mathbf{d}}_T\}$ with $\tilde{\mathbf{d}} = (f, \mathbf{b}, \mathbf{o})$ is solved using a two-stage process which utilizes the Hungarian algorithm [116] for global frame-to-frame data association. As all measurements are made in the image domain, it is natural to associate objects directly in the image rather than in 3D to better account for uncertainties.

Frame-to-Frame Association: First, individual frames are associated frame-by-frame in a tracking-by-detection framework. For all frames of a sequence, we associate all object detections above a certain detection score to the existing tracklets using the Hungarian algorithm [116]. If a detection has not been assigned to any of the existing tracklets, a new tracklet is spawned. The affinity matrix is computed using both geometry and appearance cues of the object. Experimentally we found that combining both cues yields the best association results possible. As geometry cue we employ the bounding box intersection over union score. The appearance cue is computed by correlating the bounding box region in the previous frame with the bounding box region in the current frame, using a small margin (20%) to account for the localization uncertainty of the object detector. Let $\tilde{\mathbf{d}}_i$ and $\tilde{\mathbf{d}}_j$ denote two object detections in consecutive frames. Then, the (i, j)'th entry of the affinity matrix $\mathbf{A}$ is given by

$$A_{i,j} = \begin{cases} \Gamma(\tilde{\mathbf{d}}_i, \tilde{\mathbf{d}}_j) & \text{if } \Gamma(\tilde{\mathbf{d}}_i, \tilde{\mathbf{d}}_j) < \tau_{t1} \\ \infty & \text{otherwise} \end{cases} \quad (4.1)$$

$$\Gamma(\tilde{\mathbf{d}}_i, \tilde{\mathbf{d}}_j) = \left(1 - \frac{box(\tilde{\mathbf{d}}_i) \cap box(\tilde{\mathbf{d}}_j)}{box(\tilde{\mathbf{d}}_i) \cup box(\tilde{\mathbf{d}}_j)}\right) \times \left(1 - xcorr(\tilde{\mathbf{d}}_i, \tilde{\mathbf{d}}_j)\right)$$

where $box(\cdot)$ returns the bounding box $\mathbf{b}$ that belongs to a detected object, $xcorr(\cdot, \cdot)$ returns the maximum of the normalized cross-correlation of two detections, and τ_{t1} is the gating threshold of stage one. The optimal assignment given the affinity matrix A_{ij} can be efficiently computed in polynomial time using the Kuhn-Munkres algorithm [116], yielding a set of initial tracklets.

Tracklet-to-Tracklet Association: So far, only adjacent object detections have been considered. In practice, however, it occurs quite frequently that object detections are missing for a couple of frames. This may be caused by imperfections of the object detector, or simply by the fact that other objects like cars, pedestrians or traffic signs occlude the target of interest. Yet, longer tracklets provide more information to our model than short tracklets. Thus we employ a second association stage where we associate tracklets with each other which may be occluded for up to 20 contiguous frames. Similar to the problem above we make use of the Hungarian algorithm for optimal data association, but this time we associate tracklets instead of detections and consider the whole sequence at once. Each entry of the association matrix refers to a pair of tracklets within the whole sequence. The affinity matrix $\mathbf{A}$ is given by

$$A_{i,j} = \begin{cases} \Gamma(\tilde{\mathbf{t}}_i, \tilde{\mathbf{t}}_j) & \text{if } f_\Delta(\tilde{\mathbf{t}}_i, \tilde{\mathbf{t}}_j) < N \wedge \Gamma(\tilde{\mathbf{t}}_i, \tilde{\mathbf{t}}_j) < \tau_{t2} \\ \infty & \text{otherwise} \end{cases} \quad (4.2)$$
$$\Gamma(\tilde{\mathbf{t}}_i, \tilde{\mathbf{t}}_j) = \min\left(dist(\tilde{\mathbf{t}}_i, \tilde{\mathbf{t}}_j), dist(\tilde{\mathbf{t}}_j, \tilde{\mathbf{t}}_i)\right) \times \left(1 - xcorr(\tilde{\mathbf{t}}_i, \tilde{\mathbf{t}}_j)\right)$$

where $f_\Delta(\cdot, \cdot)$ returns the frame gap between tracklets and $dist(\cdot, \cdot)$ extrapolates the bounding boxes of each tracklet linearly to predict the bounding boxes of the other tracklet and returns the mean of the normalized prediction errors with respect to the bounding box location, width and height. Extrapolation is carried out by linear regression, i.e., we fit lines to the bounding box location, width and height, where each of these modalities is considered a function of the frame number. We also experimented with higher-order prediction schemes, but found a decrease in performance due to the large and correlated noise in our measurements. Similar to above, $xcorr(\cdot, \cdot)$ compares object appearances via the normalized cross-correlation score, but this time maximized over all possible combinations of object detections within $\tilde{\mathbf{t}}_i$ and $\tilde{\mathbf{t}}_j$. We found that this procedure to significantly alleviate the effect of semi-occlusions and moderate appearance changes and leads to longer and more stable tracklet associations. The gating threshold of stage two is denoted by τ_{t2}.

4.1.3. Projection into 3D

While the object detection and object tracking stages in Section 4.1.1 and Section 4.1.2 operate directly in the 2D image domain $(\tilde{\mathbf{t}})$, the proposed intersection model reasons about tracklets in 3D $(\mathbf{t})$. In order to extract 3D information, we make the following two observations:

- Intersections are typically flat and can be well approximated using a single ground plane, which is easily and robustly extracted from structure-from-motion point clouds or disparity maps. For an overview on plane-fitting methods, the reader is referred to [39, 169, 201, 62]. As cars are driving on the ground, the bounding box contact point (bottom of the bounding box) in combination with an estimate of the ground plane can be employed to 'triangulate' the 3D location of the object.

- Given the 2D bounding box and the 3D dimensions of an object, its distance can be estimated. Hereto, we learn the statistics of cars from bounding boxes and disparity images using a held-out car dataset and back-propagate the location and its uncertainty into 3D.

Both ideas are illustrated in Fig. 4.3 and detailed in the following. Let $\varphi : \mathbf{b} \to \mathbf{m}, \mathbf{S}$ be a mapping which takes an object bounding box $\mathbf{b} \in \mathbb{R}^4$ as input and maps it to a 3D location $(x, z)^\mathsf{T} \sim \mathcal{N}(\mathbf{m}, \mathbf{S})$ on the road surface, where $\mathbf{m}$ is the mean and $\mathbf{S}$ denotes the covariance matrix. Again, 3D refers to the bird's eye perspective ($y = 0$ plane in

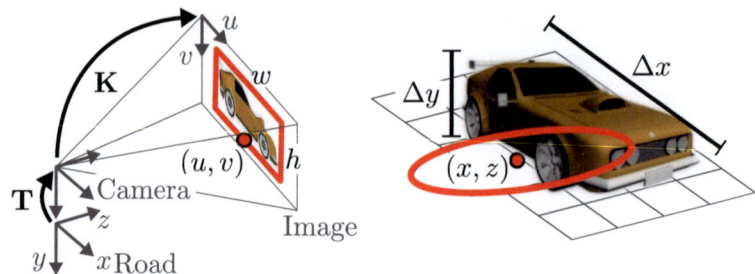

Figure 4.3.: **Projection of 2D Object Detections into 3D.** Assuming known calibration parameters $\mathbf{K}$, a rigid 3D ground plane transformation $\mathbf{T}$ and knowledge about typical object dimensions $(\Delta x, \Delta y)$, the 3D location (x, z) can be estimated from the bounding box size (w, h) and ground contact point (u, v).

road coordinates) as we are making a ground plane assumption, i.e. we assume that all objects are attached to and move on a common ground plane. Let us further assume that the mapping is probabilistic. As cues for this mapping we use the location of the bounding box ground contact point as well as the bounding box width and height. The unknown parameters of the mapping are the uncertainty in bounding box location σ_u, σ_v and size σ_w, σ_h as well as the real-world object dimensions $\Delta x, \Delta y$ and their uncertainties $\sigma_{\Delta x}, \sigma_{\Delta y}$. All parameters are learned from a held out training dataset with annotated bounding boxes and depth from stereo.

More formally, let $(u, v)^\mathsf{T}$ denote the image coordinates of the bottom-center point of the object's bounding box and let w, h be the width and height of the bounding box. Let $(x, 0, z)^\mathsf{T}$ be the 3D location of an object in ground plane coordinates ($y = 0$) as illustrated in Fig. 4.3. Further, let $\Delta x, \Delta y$ be the object width and height in meters, measured via parallel-projection to the plane $z = 0$, which is coplanar to the image plane. Finally, let o denote the MAP orientation of the vehicle as returned by the object detector.

The posterior on the object's 3D location is factorized as

$$
\begin{aligned}
&p(x, z | u, v, w, h, \Delta x, \Delta y, o) \\
&\propto p(u, v, w, h | x, z, \Delta x, \Delta y, o) p(x, z) \\
&= p(u, v | x, z, \Delta x, \Delta y, o) \, p(w | x, z, \Delta x, \Delta y, o) \\
&\quad \times p(h | x, z, \Delta x, \Delta y, o) \\
&= p(u, v | x, z) \, p(w | z, \Delta x, o) \, p(h | z, \Delta y) \\
&\propto p(x, z | u, v) \, p(z | w, \Delta x, o) \, p(z | h, \Delta y)
\end{aligned}
\tag{4.3}
$$

where we have assumed a uniform prior over x and z. The first term on the right hand side of Eq. 4.3 relates the bounding box ground contact point $(u, v)^\mathsf{T}$ to the object's 3D location $(x, 0, z)^\mathsf{T}$. The second and the last term model the relationship between the distance z of the object to the observer and the bounding box width w and height h, respectively. Note that the term $p(z | w, \Delta x, o)$ which models the width Δx in terms of parallel projection to the $z = 0$ plane depends on the object orientation o. This is because the width of a vehicle differs from its length, thus we learn a separate set of statistics for each object orientation. However, for clarity of presentation the dependency on o will be dropped in the following. Let

$$
x, z | u, v \sim \mathcal{N}(\boldsymbol{\mu}_1, \boldsymbol{\Lambda}_1^{-1})
\tag{4.4}
$$

$$
z | w, \Delta x \sim \mathcal{N}(\mu_2, \lambda_2^{-2})
\tag{4.5}
$$

$$
z | h, \Delta y \sim \mathcal{N}(\mu_3, \lambda_3^{-2})
\tag{4.6}
$$

Then, from Eq. 4.3 we have $x, z | u, v, w, h, \Delta x, \Delta y \sim \mathcal{N}(\mathbf{m}, \mathbf{S})$ with

$$
\begin{aligned}
\mathbf{m} &= \mathbf{S}\boldsymbol{\Lambda}_1\boldsymbol{\mu}_1 + \mathbf{S}\boldsymbol{\Lambda}_2 \begin{bmatrix} 0 \\ \mu_2 \end{bmatrix} + \mathbf{S}\boldsymbol{\Lambda}_3 \begin{bmatrix} 0 \\ \mu_3 \end{bmatrix} \\
\mathbf{S} &= (\boldsymbol{\Lambda}_1 + \boldsymbol{\Lambda}_2 + \boldsymbol{\Lambda}_3)^{-1}
\end{aligned}
\tag{4.7}
$$

where $\mathbf{\Lambda}_1$ has full rank and $\mathbf{\Lambda}_2, \mathbf{\Lambda}_3$ are singular matrices of the form

$$\mathbf{\Lambda}_2 = \begin{bmatrix} 0 & 0 \\ 0 & \lambda_2 \end{bmatrix} \qquad \mathbf{\Lambda}_3 = \begin{bmatrix} 0 & 0 \\ 0 & \lambda_3 \end{bmatrix} \qquad (4.8)$$

The individual feature cues are described in the following.

Ground Contact Point: Let $x, z | u, v \sim \mathcal{N}(\boldsymbol{\mu}_1, \mathbf{\Lambda}_1^{-1})$ and let us assume a standard pinhole camera model which projects a 3D ground plane point $(x, 0, z)^\mathsf{T}$ to the point $(u, v)^\mathsf{T}$ on the image plane. In homogeneous coordinates, this projection can be written as

$$\begin{bmatrix} u \\ v \\ 1 \end{bmatrix} = \mathbf{P}^{3 \times 4} \begin{bmatrix} x \\ 0 \\ z \\ 1 \end{bmatrix} \qquad (4.9)$$

where $\mathbf{P} = \mathbf{K} \mathbf{T} \mathbf{R}$ is the product of a calibration matrix $\mathbf{K}^{3 \times 3}$, the transformation from ground plane coordinates to camera coordinates $\mathbf{T}^{3 \times 4}$ (estimated a-priori) and an additional camera pitch error θ, parameterized by the rotation matrix

$$\mathbf{R}^{4 \times 4}(\theta) = \begin{bmatrix} 0 & 0 & 0 & 0 \\ 0 & \cos\theta & -\sin\theta & 0 \\ 0 & \sin\theta & \cos\theta & 0 \\ 0 & 0 & 0 & 1 \end{bmatrix} \qquad (4.10)$$

Given $(u, v)^\mathsf{T}$ we obtain $\boldsymbol{\mu}_1 = (x, z)^\mathsf{T}$ by solving the linear system

$$\mathbf{A} \begin{bmatrix} x \\ z \end{bmatrix} = \mathbf{b} \qquad (4.11)$$

with

$$\begin{aligned} \mathbf{A} &= \begin{bmatrix} uP_{31} - P_{11} & u(P_{33}\cos\theta - P_{32}\sin\theta) - (P_{13}\cos\theta - P_{12}\sin\theta) \\ vP_{31} - P_{21} & v(P_{33}\cos\theta - p_{32}\sin\theta) - (P_{23}\cos\theta - P_{22}\sin\theta) \end{bmatrix} \\ &= \begin{bmatrix} uP_{31} - P_{11} & uP_{33} - P_{13} \\ vP_{31} - P_{21} & vP_{33} - P_{23} \end{bmatrix} \\ \mathbf{b} &= \begin{bmatrix} P_{14} - uP_{34} \\ P_{24} - vP_{34} \end{bmatrix} \end{aligned} \tag{4.12}$$

where P_{ij} denotes the ij'th element of $\mathbf{P}$ and we have made use of $E(\theta) = 0$ as $\mathbf{R}$ only models the *error* in pitch. Assuming the covariance of $(u, v)^\mathsf{T}$ to be known, the covariance of $(x, z)^\mathsf{T}$ can be approximated using error propagation. Since the transformation implied by Eq. 4.11 is non-linear with respect to u, v and θ, we linearize it by means of a first-order Taylor expansion. Given σ_u, σ_v and σ_θ we have

$$\mathbf{\Lambda}_1 = \mathbf{\Sigma}_1^{-1} \qquad \mathbf{\Sigma}_1 = \mathbf{J} \begin{bmatrix} \sigma_u^2 & 0 & 0 \\ 0 & \sigma_v^2 & 0 \\ 0 & 0 & \sigma_\theta^2 \end{bmatrix} \mathbf{J}^\mathsf{T} \tag{4.13}$$

where the Jacobian $\mathbf{J} \in \mathbb{R}^{3\times 3}$ is given by

$$\mathbf{J} = \begin{pmatrix} \frac{\partial}{\partial u}\mathbf{A}^{-1}\mathbf{b} & \frac{\partial}{\partial v}\mathbf{A}^{-1}\mathbf{b} & \frac{\partial}{\partial\theta}\mathbf{A}^{-1}\mathbf{b} \end{pmatrix} \tag{4.14}$$

with

$$\begin{aligned} \partial(\mathbf{A}^{-1}\mathbf{b}) &= \partial\mathbf{A}^{-1}\mathbf{b} + \mathbf{A}^{-1}\partial\mathbf{b} \\ &= -\mathbf{A}^{-1}\partial\mathbf{A}\mathbf{A}^{-1}\mathbf{b} + \mathbf{A}^{-1}\partial\mathbf{b} \\ &= \mathbf{A}^{-1}\left(\partial\mathbf{b} - \partial\mathbf{A}\mathbf{A}^{-1}\mathbf{b}\right) \end{aligned} \tag{4.15}$$

and

$$\frac{\partial}{\partial u}\mathbf{A} = \begin{bmatrix} P_{31} & P_{33} \\ 0 & 0 \end{bmatrix} \quad \frac{\partial}{\partial u}\mathbf{b} = \begin{bmatrix} -P_{34} \\ 0 \end{bmatrix}$$

$$\frac{\partial}{\partial v}\mathbf{A} = \begin{bmatrix} 0 & 0 \\ P_{31} & P_{33} \end{bmatrix} \quad \frac{\partial}{\partial v}\mathbf{b} = \begin{bmatrix} 0 \\ -P_{34} \end{bmatrix} \quad (4.16)$$

$$\frac{\partial}{\partial \theta}\mathbf{A} = \begin{bmatrix} 0 & P_{12} - uP_{32} \\ 0 & P_{22} - vP_{32} \end{bmatrix} \quad \frac{\partial}{\partial \theta}\mathbf{b} = \begin{bmatrix} 0 \\ 0 \end{bmatrix}$$

Object Width: As state above, we assume $z|w, \Delta x, o \sim \mathcal{N}(\mu_2, \sigma_2^2)$. From the pinhole model we obtain the relationship

$$w = \frac{f\Delta x}{z} \quad (4.17)$$

with f the focal length, or equivalently

$$\mu_2 = z = \frac{f\Delta x}{w} \quad (4.18)$$

which is a non-linear function in w. Using the same reasoning as above, we obtain the variance in z through error propagation as

$$\lambda_2 = \sigma_2^{-2} \quad \sigma_2^2 = \mathbf{J} \begin{bmatrix} \sigma_w^2 & 0 \\ 0 & \sigma_{\Delta x}^2 \end{bmatrix} \mathbf{J}^\mathsf{T} \quad (4.19)$$

with Jacobian

$$\mathbf{J} = \begin{bmatrix} -\frac{f\Delta x}{w^2} & \frac{f}{w} \end{bmatrix} \quad (4.20)$$

In order to properly account for the viewing angle represented by a set of discrete object orientation classes o, we learn a separate set of parameters (μ_2, σ_2^2) for each o as illustrated in Fig. 4.4 and 4.5.

Object Height: Similarly to the object width term, we assume a Gaussian distribution $z|h, \Delta y \sim \mathcal{N}(\mu_3, \sigma_3^2)$ for the object height term. We obtain

$$\mu_3 = z = \frac{f\Delta y}{h} \tag{4.21}$$

with variance

$$\lambda_3 = \sigma_3^{-2} \qquad \sigma_3^2 = \mathbf{J} \begin{bmatrix} \sigma_h^2 & 0 \\ 0 & \sigma_{\Delta y}^2 \end{bmatrix} \mathbf{J}^\mathsf{T} \tag{4.22}$$

and Jacobian

$$\mathbf{J} = \begin{bmatrix} -\frac{f\Delta y}{h^2} & \frac{f}{h} \end{bmatrix} \tag{4.23}$$

Note that the height does not depend on the object heading o.

Learning the Parameters of the 3D Projection Model: The unknown parameters of the proposed projection model σ_u, σ_v, σ_w, σ_h, Δx, Δy, $\sigma_{\Delta x}$ and $\sigma_{\Delta y}$ are learned automatically from annotated training data. For this purpose we have collected a dataset of 1020 images that capture 3634 vehicles with annotated 2D bounding boxes and computed the corresponding disparity maps. The labels do not only include the bounding box but also the heading of the vehicles, quantized into 8 orientations $o \in \{1, \ldots, 8\}$. This is important as the object width depends on the orientation of the vehicle.

We first estimate the parameters related to detection accuracy σ_u, σ_v, σ_w and σ_h by comparing the object detections with the manually labeled 2D bounding boxes. Due to the characteristics of sliding-window detectors, we expect the noise to be dependent on the object scale. A good approximation to object scale is the bounding box height h as in contrast to the bounding box width it is largely invariant with respect to the viewing angle. Furthermore, it is readily given by the object detector. Figure 4.4 depicts σ_u, σ_v, σ_w and σ_h as a function of h. As the noise σ depends approximately linearly on h it can be well represented via the linear model

$$\sigma_x(h) = a_{x,o}\, h + b_{x,o} \tag{4.24}$$

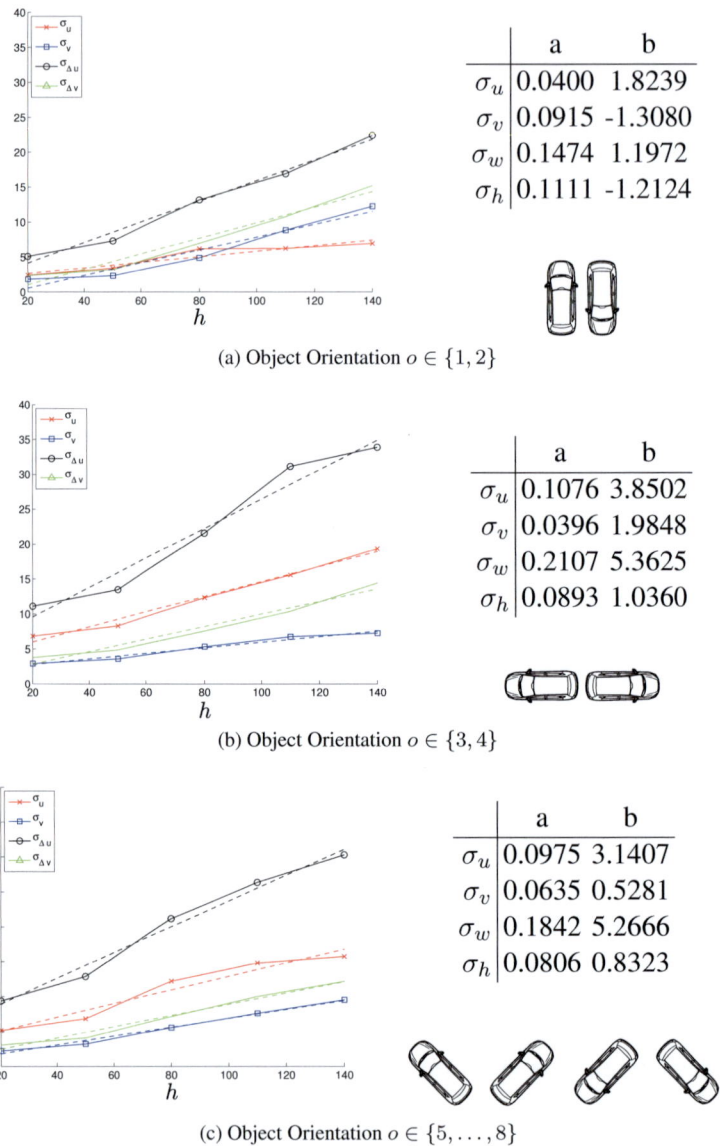

(a) Object Orientation $o \in \{1, 2\}$

(b) Object Orientation $o \in \{3, 4\}$

(c) Object Orientation $o \in \{5, \ldots, 8\}$

Figure 4.4.: **Bounding Box Uncertainty.** This figure illustrates the linear relationship between the error of the object detector and the object size (height h) for the 3 object orientation classes.

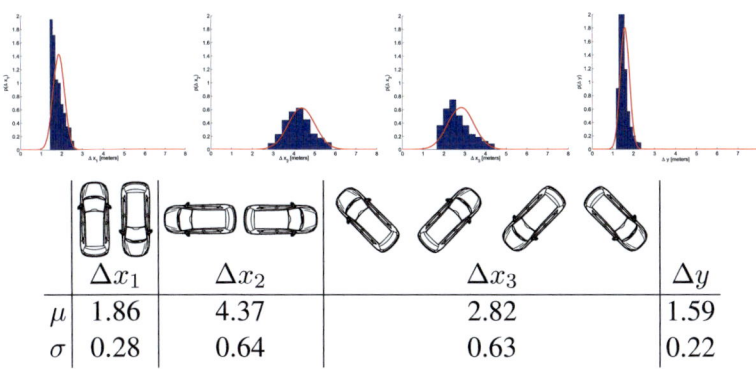

	Δx_1	Δx_2	Δx_3	Δy
μ	1.86	4.37	2.82	1.59
σ	0.28	0.64	0.63	0.22

Figure 4.5.: **Object Size Statistics.** Cars in our dataset are $\sim$ 1.9m wide and $\sim$ 4.4m long. Here, Δx and Δy are the width and height of the object after parallel projection onto the $z = 0$ plane, with z the optical axis.

with $x \in \{u, v, w, h\}$. Here, a and b are obtained using least squares estimation. The parameters describing the real-world dimensions of the object's parallel projection to the $z = 0$ plane are Δx, Δy, $\sigma_{\Delta x}$ and $\sigma_{\Delta y}$. They are obtained from the annotated data in conjunction with the stereo information. Given a rectified stereo camera rig, the following relations hold:

$$\Delta x = \frac{zw}{f} = \frac{bw}{d} \qquad \Delta y = \frac{zh}{f} = \frac{bh}{d} \qquad (4.25)$$

Here, z is the distance of the object to the camera, f denotes the camera's focal length, b is the camera baseline and d represents the median disparity within the 2D bounding box. As noted above, special care has to be taken for Δx as it depends on the orientation of the object. We learn a separate Δx for each of three car orientation classes illustrated in Fig. 4.4. The results are depicted in Fig. 4.5. When viewed frontally or from behind a typical car is $\sim$ 1.9 meters wide. It spans $\sim$ 4.4 meters when viewed from the side. The resulting posterior probabilities for 3 tracklet detections are illustrated in

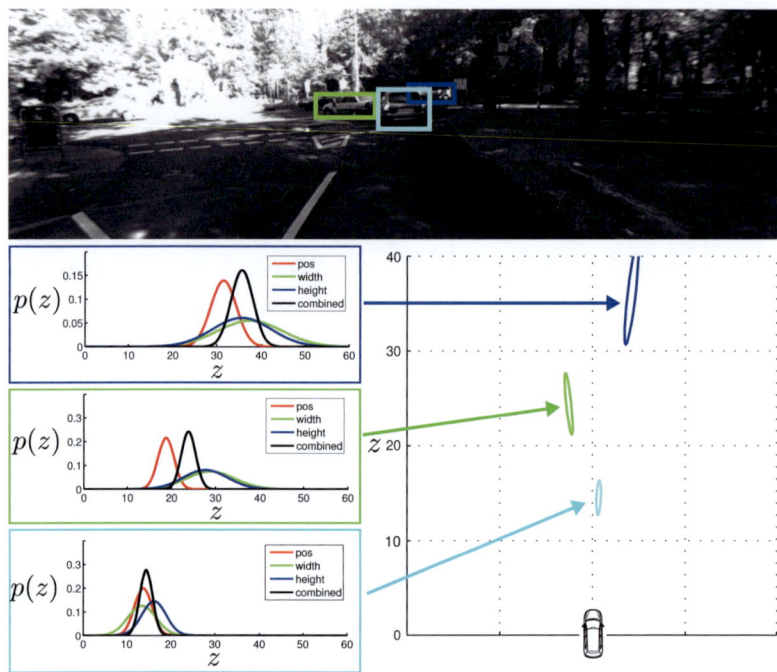

Figure 4.6.: **Depth Posterior Distribution.** This figure depicts the marginal depth distributions for each feature cue individually (red,green,blue) and the posterior distribution (black) when combining the results using Eq. 4.3.

Fig. 4.6. The colored curves are the individual cues discussed in the previous sections and the black curves depict the combined posterior results.

4.1.4. Temporal Integration

As the raw 3D location estimates $\{(\mathbf{m}, \mathbf{S})\}$ are noisy due to the low camera viewpoint, the uncertainties in the object detector and the ground plane estimation process, we temporally integrate detections within a tracklet $\mathbf{t}$ using a Kalman smoother [105] assuming a

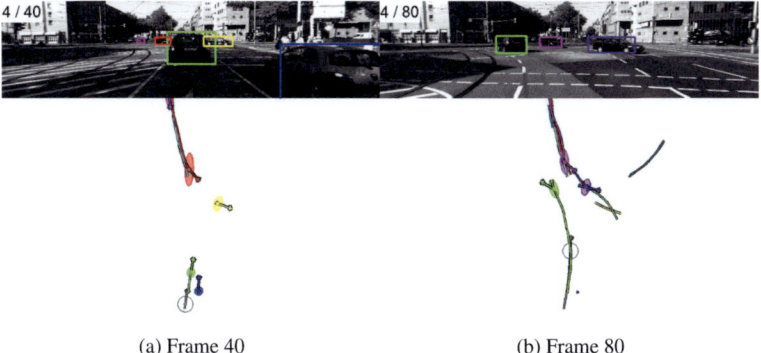

(a) Frame 40   (b) Frame 80

Figure 4.7.: **Filtered 3D Vehicle Tracklets.** This figure shows two frames of a crossing sequence. The top row depicts the input image with the detected objects and the bottom row shows the 3D tracklets in bird's eye perspective after smoothing. The covariance ellipsoids are shown for the current frame. The gray trajectory is generated by the moving observer. The top-right tracklet is caused by outlier detections from the tipper at the right side of the image.

constant velocity model. This step finally yields the tracklet observations which are augmented by the frame number f_d and the object orientation distribution o_d to tracklets $t = \{d_1, \ldots, d_{M_d}\}$ with $d = (f_d, m_d, S_d, o_d)$ and serve as input to our probabilistic model in Section 3.3.2. An illustration of the estimated 3D tracklets is provided in Fig. 4.7, where the covariance ellipses depict the uncertainty in object location.

4.2. Vanishing Points

Vanishing points are good street orientation cues as image gradients from road markings or buildings are often aligned with the dominant streets. For example, in Fig. 1.2 the forward facing street is well supported by the curbstones. In many cases, the crossing street is supported by road markings, windows or building outlines as well.

Figure 4.8.: **Vanishing Points.** For each scene, we detect up to two dominant vanishing points, one corresponding to the forward-facing street (shown in green with vanishing lines in red) and one corresponding to the crossing street (vanishing lines in blue, the corresponding vanishing point is located outside of the image).

We detect up to $N_v = 2$ vanishing points $\mathcal{V} = \{v_1, \ldots, v_{N_v}\}$, where a vanishing point is defined by a rotation angle around the y-axis in road coordinates, i.e. we assume that all vanishing lines are collinear with the ground plane and v_i represents their yaw angle. All 3D lines that are collinear with a vanishing line intersect at the same vanishing point. For typical scenarios, two vanishing points are dominant: One which is collinear with the forward facing street and one which is collinear with the crossing street. The vertical vanishing points are not informative.

In order to detect vanishing points we first extract long line segments. Towards this goal we make use of the method described by Kosecka et al. [114], which detects long lines in the image by Canny edge detection [35] followed by labeling the connected orientation components and fitting the line parameters using principal component analysis. Given the line segments, we detect vanishing points similarly to [114], but taking into account the (known) camera calibration information and restricting the search space such that all vanishing lines are collinear with the ground plane. Additionally, we relax the model to also allow for non-orthogonal vanishing points as this is required by the intersection types in our dataset.

Unfortunately, traditional vanishing point detection methods [114,

15] require relatively clean scenarios and tend to fail in the presence of clutter such as cast shadows on a sunny day, railway tracks or defects in the road surface that easily mislead the vanishing point detection process. To tackle this problem, we learn a k-nearest-neighbor classifier based on a held-out annotated set of 185 images, in which all detected line segments have been manually labeled as either *structure* or *clutter*. Here, *structure* refers to the line segments of interest, which are aligned with the major orientations of the streets or building facades. The classifier's confidence on *structure* is used as a weight in the vanishing point voting process.

The feature set for classification comprises multiple types of information: As geometric information the position, length and orientation of the line are included. Further, we incorporate context knowledge by counting the number of lines with similar and perpendicular orientation in a local window around the target pixel. The local appearance is represented by the mean, standard deviation and entropy of all pixels, computed over a small margin of 3 pixels at both sides of the line. Finally, we add texton-like features from a Gabor filter bank as well as the 3 principal components of the scene GIST [145].

The benefits of this additional learning step are highlighted in Fig. 4.9(a), which shows the ROC curve for classifying lines into *structure* and *clutter*. The curves have been obtained by adjusting k for the k-nn classifier in the learning based method and by varying the inlier threshold for [114]. Fig. 4.9(b) compares the classification results for a particular scene: While the cast shadows in the lower-left part of the image causes wrong evidence for traditional vanishing point detectors [114] (top), the proposed classification step is able to reject most of those line segments (bottom).

Applying the restricted version of [114] to all structured line segments and thresholding yields up to $N_v = 2$ vanishing points $\mathcal{V} = \{v_1, \ldots, v_{N_v}\}$ which serve as input to the vanishing point likelihood in Section 3.3.3.

67

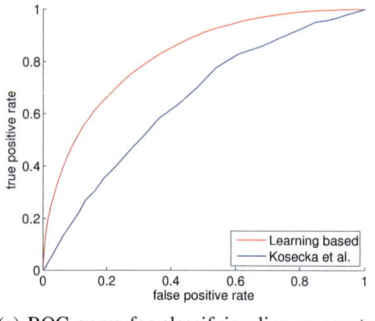 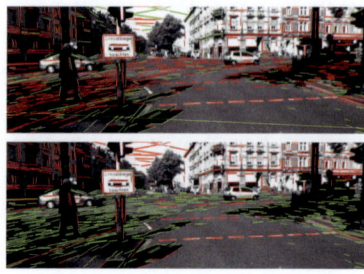

(a) ROC curve for classifying line segments into *structure* and *clutter*.

(b) Kosecka et al. (top) vs. proposed approach (bottom). Red corresponds to *structure*.

Figure 4.9.: **Structured Line Segments.** As cast shadows and road defects generate a lot of structured line segments which can easily confuse the vanishing point estimation process, we classify each detected line into *structural information* versus *clutter*.

4.3. Semantic Scene Labels

The appearance of objects and what is often referred to as 'stuff' in the computer vision literature (i.e., objects without extend such as sky road or vegetation) provides additional cues about the layout of the scene. For example, the texture statistics of road area usually differs from the statistics of building or sky. Furthermore, geometric priors can be taken into account, e.g. buildings are located above the road and below the sky. We can make use of this information by comparing a semantic segmentation of the scene to a projection of our model into the image. See Fig. 3.4 and Fig. 4.10 for an illustration.

For extracting semantic information in the form of scene labels we use the joint boosting framework proposed in [180] to learn a strong classifier. Following Wojek et al. [191], we divide the last image of each sequence into patches of size $n_s \times n_s$ pixels and classify them into the categories *road*, *background* and *sky*. In order to avoid hard decisions and to interpret the boosting confidences as probabilities

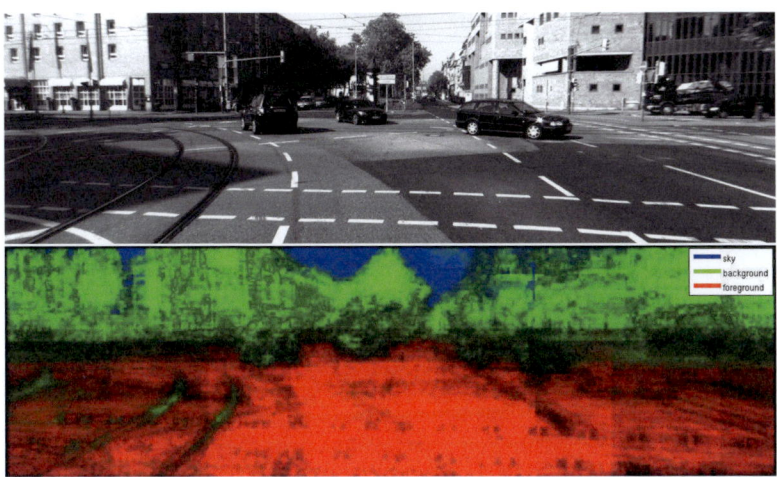

Figure 4.10.: **Semantic Image Segmentation.** We learn a classifier to compute per-pixel likelihoods for the classes *sky*, *background* and *foreground*.

we apply the softmax transformation [119] to the resulting scores. The semantic label of a single patch is defined as $\mathbf{s} \in \Delta^2$, where Δ^2 is the unit 2-simplex as described in Section 3.2. We make use of the following features for classification:

- Generic texture cues are computed from the first 16 coefficients of the Walsh-Hadamard transform [2], which is a discrete approximation to the cosine transformation and has been shown to perform well in practice [191] on sequences similar to the ones used in this work.

- As urban scenes contain many man-made structures we include the feature set for man-made structure detection described by Kumar et al. [118, 117] on patches of size 16×16, 32×32 and 64×64 pixels.

- Finally, the image location is incorporated by concatenating the pixel coordinates to the feature vector. This enables to

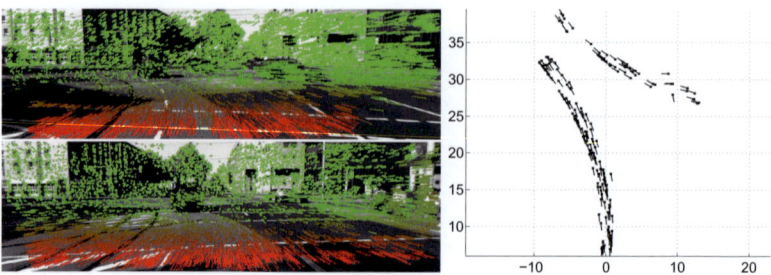

Figure 4.11.: **Scene Flow.** By matching features between the left and right images of a stereo pair and over time, we obtain 3D flow vectors (left). Color codes disparity from large (red) to small (green) values. When compensating the egomotion the dynamic parts of the scene can be extracted and accumulated in a common coordinate system (right, bird's eye view).

encode knowledge such as the sky being located on top and the road at the bottom of the image.

For training, we use a hold out dataset of 200 hand-labeled images. Fig. 4.10 illustrates the results of the proposed semantic image feature cue on one of the test images from our database. After softmax normalization we obtain a (discrete) scene label distribution s for each image patch $s \in \mathcal{S}$, which is used in our semantic scene label likelihood described in Section 3.3.4.

4.4. Scene Flow

Due to the low viewpoint of the car-mounted camera depth information is very noisy when only relying on monocular feature cues. Thus, we also investigate the use of stereo features, which are described in this and the following section. Note that even for stereo features the depth error increases quadratically with the distance. However, due to the different noise properties a gain in performance can be expected when properly combining stereo and monocular cues, which we verify in the experimental section of this thesis.

The first feature cue we pursue here is the 3D scene flow caused by moving traffic participants. The observation is that most of the non-background motion in the scene is caused by vehicles following a street or crossing the intersection. Assuming right-handed traffic and that the majority of traffic participants keep up with the traffic rules, these flow vectors should be explained by the underlying scene model, i.e. all vehicles are driving on the correct lanes into the right direction.

Towards extracting 3D scene flow vectors $\mathbf{f}$, we first extract feature matches from the image sequence. In order to find stable feature locations, we filter the input images with 5×5 blob and corner masks as illustrated in Fig. 4.12(a). Next, we employ non-maximum- and non-minimum-suppression [143] on the filtered images, resulting in feature candidates which belong to one of four classes (i.e., blob max, blob min, corner max, corner min). To reduce computational efforts, only features within those classes are matched.

In contrast to methods concerned with reconstructions from un-ordered image collections, here we assume a smooth camera trajec-tory, superseding computationally intense rotation and scale invari-ant feature descriptors like SURF [18, 17], SIFT [134, 135] or others [34, 33, 158, 132]. We compute a compact 32 byte feature descriptor from the 8 bit quantized horizontal and vertical Sobel responses at the 16 locations shown in Fig. 4.12(b). Since the sum-of-absolute-differences of 16 bytes can be computed very efficiently using a sin-gle SSE instruction we only need two calls in order to evaluate this error metric.

We match features between the left and right images and between two consecutive frames. This is achieved by matching features in a 'circle': Starting from all feature candidates in the *current left* image, we find the best match in the *previous left* image within a $M \times M$ search window, next in the *previous right* image, the *current right* image and last in the *current left* image again. A 'circle match' gets accepted, if the last feature index coincides with the first feature in-dex. When matching between the left and right images, we addition-

71

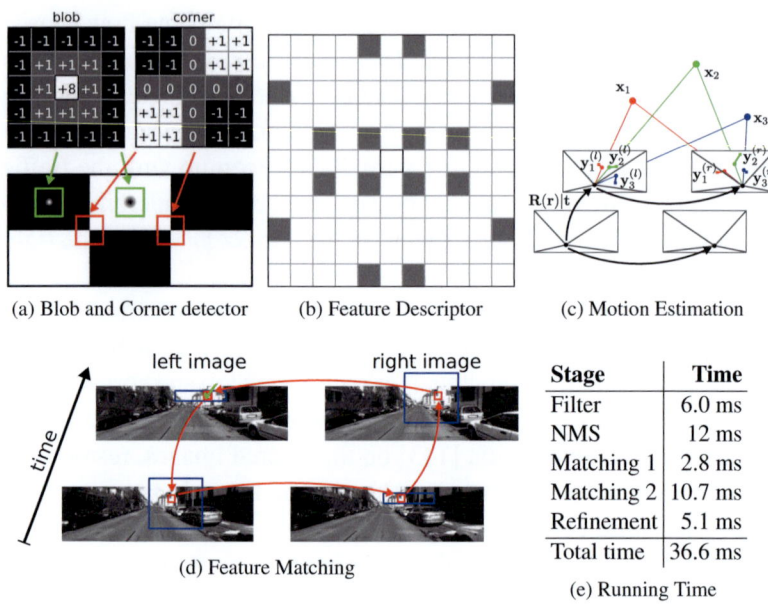

(a) Blob and Corner detector   (b) Feature Descriptor   (c) Motion Estimation

(d) Feature Matching

Stage	Time
Filter	6.0 ms
NMS	12 ms
Matching 1	2.8 ms
Matching 2	10.7 ms
Refinement	5.1 ms
Total time	36.6 ms

(e) Running Time

Figure 4.12.: **Feature Matching and Egomotion Estimation.** Blob and corner features are detected with filters (a), described using Sobel filter responses arranged in a star-like shape (b) and matched in two consecutive stereo pairs (d). Egomotion is obtained using the 3-point algorithm (c). Running times are given in (e).

ally make use of the epipolar constraint using an error tolerance of 1 pixel. For further details[3], the reader is referred to [75].

Given all 'circular' feature matches from the previous section, we compute the camera motion by minimizing the sum of re-projection errors using the 3-point algorithm [144, 47, 85]. First, bucketing [110] is applied to reduce the number of features (in practice we retain between 200 and 500 features) and spread them uniformly over the image domain. Next, we project the feature points from the previous frame into 3D via triangulation using the calibration parameters

---

[3]Source code available at: http://www.mrt.kit.edu/software/

of the stereo camera rig. Assuming squared pixels and zero skew, the reprojection into the current image is given by

$$
\begin{pmatrix} u \\ v \\ 1 \end{pmatrix} = \begin{pmatrix} f & 0 & c_u \\ 0 & f & c_v \\ 0 & 0 & 1 \end{pmatrix} \left[[\mathbf{R}(\mathbf{r}), \mathbf{t}] \begin{pmatrix} x \\ y \\ z \\ 1 \end{pmatrix} - \begin{pmatrix} s \\ 0 \\ 0 \end{pmatrix} \right]
\tag{4.26}
$$

with

- homogeneous image coordinates $(u \ v \ 1)^\mathsf{T}$

- focal length f

- principal point (c_u, c_v)

- rotation matrix $\mathbf{R}(\mathbf{r}) = \mathbf{R}_x(r_x)\mathbf{R}_y(r_y)\mathbf{R}_z(r_z)$

- rotation vector $\mathbf{t} = (r_x \ r_y \ r_z)^\mathsf{T}$

- translation vector $\mathbf{t} = (t_x \ t_y \ t_z)^\mathsf{T}$

- 3D coordinates $\mathbf{x} = (x \ y \ z)^\mathsf{T}$

- and shift $s = 0$ (left image) or $s =$ baseline (right image)

Let now $\pi_l(\mathbf{x}; \mathbf{r}, \mathbf{t}) : \mathbb{R}^3 \to \mathbb{R}^2$ denote the projection implied by Eq. 4.26, which takes a 3D point $\mathbf{x}$ and maps it onto the left image plane. Similarly, let $\pi_r(\mathbf{x}; \mathbf{r}, \mathbf{t})$ be the projection onto the right image plane. Using Gauss-Newton optimization, we iteratively minimize

$$
\hat{\mathbf{r}}, \hat{\mathbf{t}} - \underset{\mathbf{r}, \mathbf{t}}{\arg\min} \sum_{i=1}^{N} \left\| \mathbf{y}_i^{(l)} - \pi_l(\mathbf{x}_i; \mathbf{r}, \mathbf{t}) \right\|^2 + \left\| \mathbf{y}_i^{(r)} - \pi_r(\mathbf{x}_i; \mathbf{r}, \mathbf{t}) \right\|^2
\tag{4.27}
$$

for the rigid motion parameters $\mathbf{r}$ and $\mathbf{t}$. Here, $\mathbf{y}_i^{(l)}$ and $\mathbf{y}_i^{(r)}$ denote the feature locations in the current left and right images and $\mathbf{x}_i$ are the triangulated 3D points from the previous frame. The required Jacobians are readily derived from Eq. 4.26. In practice, even a simple initialization ($r_0 = t_0 = 0$) proved sufficient to converge in only a couple of iterations (4-8). For robustness with respect to outliers, we wrap the estimation approach into a RANSAC scheme [62]: We first estimate $(\hat{r}, \hat{t})$ n_f times independently using 3 randomly drawn correspondences. Afterwards, all inliers of the winning iteration are used for refining the parameters, yielding the final transformation parameters $(\hat{r}, \hat{t})$. While more sophisticated methods for structure and motion estimation could be employed [121, 122], we found the aforementioned procedure to be simple and accurate enough for our purpose.

The final step is to compensate the 3D scene flow vectors using the egomotion given by the transformation parameters $\{(\hat{r}, \hat{t})\}$ over time. Towards this goal, we accumulate all vectors in the coordinate system of the last frame of the sequence and threshold them by their length, i.e., we remove short vectors that are likely to belong to the static environment. As the 3D scene flow likelihood doesn't account for object velocities, we normalize all flow vectors to unit length and project them onto the estimated road plane as illustrated in Fig. 4.11 (right), yielding the scene flow features $\mathcal{F} = \{f_1, \ldots, f_{N_f}\}$ which are modeled by the scene flow likelihood in Section 3.3.5.

4.5. Occupancy Grid

Buildings represent obstacles in the scene and thus should never coincide with drivable regions (road). This assumption is incorporated into the occupancy grid feature. We construct a 2D voxel grid in road plane coordinates from disparity measurements. The grid classifies the area in front of the vehicle into the categories *obstacle, free space* and *unobserved* segments as illustrated in Fig. 4.13.

For stereo matching we propose the efficient large-scale stereo matcher ELAS[4] [73], that is capable of computing disparity maps at large image resolutions in real-time on the CPU. The method is

---

[4]Source code available at: http://www.mrt.kit.edu/software/

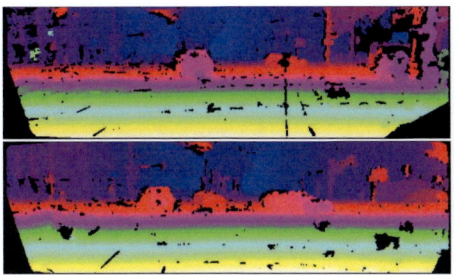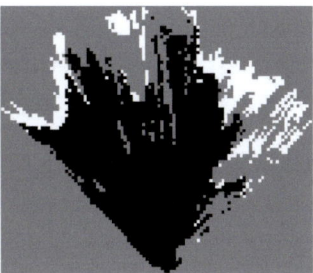

Figure 4.13.: **Occupancy Grid.** From the input disparity maps of a T-intersection (left), we compute evidence for static *obstacles* and *free space* in bird's eye view, and accumulate it over time in a common coordinate system (right, top view). Here, white denotes *obstacle*, black is *free space* and gray represents *unobserved* areas.

inspired from the observation that despite the fact that many stereo correspondences are highly ambiguous, some of them can be robustly matched. Assuming piecewise smooth disparities, such reliable 'support points' carry valuable prior information for the estimation of the remaining, ambiguous disparities in between. First, the disparities of a sparse set of support points are computed using the full disparity range. The image coordinates of the support points are then used to create a 2D mesh via Delaunay triangulation. From the mesh, a piecewise linear prior is computed to disambiguate the matching problem and increasing the efficiency by restricting the search to a plausible subspace. The algorithm automatically determines the disparity range, can be easily parallelized and has shown impressive performance on the realistic KITTI dataset [71] and on the large-scale Middlebury benchmark [165] while at the same time achieving significant speedups with respect to competing methods. Two matching results are illustrated in Fig. 4.13 (left). For a more in-depth discussion on the algorithm, the reader is referred to [73].

Given the disparity maps for all frames of the sequence, we compute a 2D occupancy grid [178] of the environment, representing obstacles and drivable (road) areas. Using the visual odometry approach described in Section 4.4, we represent all dynamic and static features in the bird's eye perspective of the last frame's camera coordinate system.

More formally, let $\mathcal{O} = \{\rho_1, \ldots, \rho_{N_o}\}$ be the occupancy grid map with ρ_i denoting if the i'th cell is free ($\rho_i = -1$) or occupied ($\rho_i = +1$). Let the probability of an occupied grid cell be denoted by $p(\rho_i) \equiv p(\rho_i = +1)$. Further, let $\mathcal{D} = \{\mathbf{D}_1, \ldots, \mathbf{D}_T\}$ denote the set of all disparity maps, with $\mathbf{D}_i$ the disparity map of the i'th frame. Assuming the odometry estimates to be known, we are interested in computing the posterior $p(\mathcal{O}|\mathcal{D})$. To make computations tractable the individual cells are assumed to be independent conditioned on the measurements $\mathcal{D}$, yielding

$$p(\mathcal{O}|\mathcal{D}) = \prod_{i=1}^{N_o} p(\rho_i|\mathcal{D}) \tag{4.28}$$

As this is a binary static state estimation problem, the discrete Bayes filter can be applied to $p(\rho_i|\mathcal{D})$. For ease of computation and numerical stability, we follow [178] and make use of the log-odds representation

$$l(\rho|\mathcal{D}) = \log \frac{p(\rho|\mathcal{D})}{p(\neg\rho|\mathcal{D})} = \log \frac{p(\rho|\mathcal{D})}{1 - p(\rho|\mathcal{D})} \tag{4.29}$$

$$p(\rho|\mathcal{D}) = \frac{\exp l(\rho|\mathcal{D})}{1 + \exp l(\rho|\mathcal{D})} \tag{4.30}$$

where we have dropped the grid cell index i for clarity. Let $\mathcal{D}_t = \{\mathbf{D}_1, \ldots, \mathbf{D}_t\}$ denote the set of disparity observations till time t. The recursive filter update gives rise to

$$
\begin{aligned}
\frac{p(\rho|\mathcal{D}_t)}{p(\neg\rho|\mathcal{D}_t)} &= \frac{p(\mathbf{D}_t|\rho, \mathcal{D}_{t-1})p(\rho|\mathcal{D}_{t-1})}{p(\mathbf{D}_t|\neg\rho, \mathcal{D}_{t-1})p(\neg\rho|\mathcal{D}_{t-1})} \\
&= \frac{p(\mathbf{D}_t|\rho)}{p(\mathbf{D}_t|\neg\rho)} \times \frac{p(\rho|\mathcal{D}_{t-1})}{p(\neg\rho|\mathcal{D}_{t-1})}
\end{aligned} \tag{4.31}
$$

or – equivalently – in log-odds representation

$$l(\rho|\mathcal{D}_t) \ = \ l(\mathbf{D}_t|\rho) + l(\rho|\mathcal{D}_{t-1}) \qquad (4.32)$$

Here, $l(\mathbf{D}_t|\rho)$ takes the form

$$l(\mathbf{D}_t|\rho) = \begin{cases} +1 & \text{if cell } \rho \text{ is not occluded} \\ -1 & \text{if cell } \rho \text{ is occluded for} < 5\text{m} \\ 0 & \text{otherwise } (> 5\text{m}) \end{cases} \qquad (4.33)$$

where the occlusion state of a cell ρ at time t is computed by tracing rays from the camera into the direction of ρ. If an obstacle higher than 2 meters from the ground plane is hit before the cell is reached, the cell is called occluded. Note that we only assign negative log-odds to cells within a 5 meter margin as no information about the region behind an obstacle is available (gray areas in Fig. 4.13, right). The minimum height requirement alleviates the problem of clutter produced by other traffic participants which are (typically) of limited height. Ray tracing on the occupancy grid can be performed efficiently using the Bresenham algorithm [26]. The last step rounds all occupancy grid cells to $\rho \in \{-1, 0, +1\}$, yielding the final occupancy grid $\mathcal{O} = \{\rho_1, \ldots, \rho_{N_o}\}$ which is modeled with the occupancy grid likelihood from Section 3.3.6.

5. Experimental Evaluation

The dataset used in the experimental section of this thesis is part of an early version of the KITTI vision dataset [71, 70], which has been recorded from a VW Passat station wagon [68, 106] (established in the context of the SFB/Transregio 28 special research field and illustrated in Fig. 5.1) while driving around Karlsruhe, Germany. Our setup includes camera images, laser scans, high-precision GPS measurements and IMU accelerations/angular velocities from a combined GPS/IMU system. The main purpose of this dataset is to push forward the development of computer vision and robotic algorithms targeted to dynamic inner-city and freeway scenes. From the recorded data[1] we have extracted benchmarks for different tasks such as stereo, optical flow, visual odometry, SLAM, 3D object detection and 3D tracking [71]. For a review on related datasets and evaluation efforts, the reader is referred to [71].

5.1. System Setup

Our sensor setup, illustrated in Fig. 5.1, is as follows:

- 2 × PointGray Flea2 grayscale cameras (FL2-14S3M-C), 1.4 Megapixels, 1/2" Sony ICX267 CCD, global shutter

- 2 × PointGray Flea2 color cameras (FL2-14S3C-C), 1.4 Megapixels, 1/2" Sony ICX267 CCD, global shutter

- 4 × Edmund Optics lenses, 4mm, opening angle $\sim 90°$, vertical opening angle of region of interest (ROI) $\sim 35°$

---

[1]The dataset available from: http://www.mrt.kit.edu/software/datasets.html

(a) Karlsruhe, Germany   (b) Experimental Vehicle AnnieWAY (MRT/KIT)

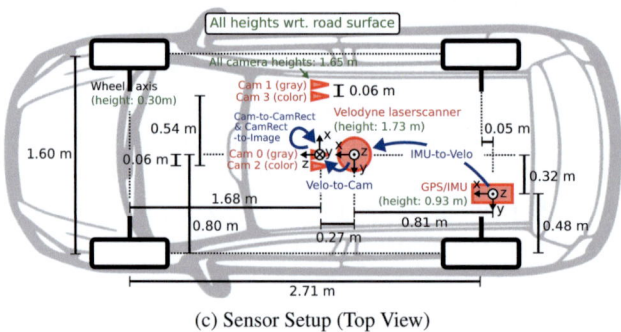

(c) Sensor Setup (Top View)

Figure 5.1.: **Recording Platform.** A VW Passat station wagon has been equipped with four video cameras (two color and two gray scale cameras). A rotating 3D laser scanner and a GPS/IMU inertial navigation system unit have been installed for obtaining ground truth annotations.

- 1 × Velodyne HDL-64E rotating 3D laser scanner, 10 Hz, 64 beams, 0.09 degree angular resolution, 2 cm distance accuracy, collecting ∼ 1.3 million points/second, field of view: 360° horizontal, 26.8° vertical, range: 120 m

- 1 × OXTS RT3003 inertial and GPS navigation system, 6 axis, 100 Hz, L1/L2 RTK, resolution: 0.02m / 0.1°

As color cameras are less sensitive to light we use two stereo camera rigs, one for grayscale and one for color. The baseline of both stereo camera rigs is approximately 54 cm and the calibration between all sensors is known. In the early setup used for the intersection subset of KITTI, we only had access to a monochrome video camera stereo rig and an GPS/IMU system for localization. The trunk of our vehicle houses a PC with two six-core Intel XEON X5650 processors and a shock-absorbed RAID 5 hard disk system, storing up to 4 terabytes. Our computer runs Ubuntu Linux (64 bit) and a database for cognitive automobiles [80] to store the incoming data streams in real-time.

5.2. Sensor Calibration

We took care that all sensors are carefully synchronized and calibrated [72, 150]. To avoid drift over time, we calibrated the sensors at each day of our recordings. The coordinate systems are defined as illustrated in Fig. 5.1, i.e.:

- Camera: x = right, y = down, z = forward

- Velodyne: x = forward, y = left, z = up

- GPS/IMU: x = forward, y = left, z = up

5.2.1. Synchronization

In order to synchronize the sensors, we use the timestamps of the Velodyne 3D laser scanner as a reference and consider each spin as a single frame. We mounted a reed contact at the bottom of the continuously rotating scanner, triggering the cameras when it is facing forward. This minimizes the differences in range and image observations caused by dynamic objects. Unfortunately, the GPS/IMU system cannot be synchronized that way. However as it provides updates at 100 Hz, we collect the data with the closest time stamp to the laser scanner time stamp for a particular frame. The remaining worst-case time difference of 5 ms can be taken into account by comparing the corresponding timestamps which are provided for each sensor modality.

5.2.2. Camera Calibration

For calibrating the cameras intrinsically and extrinsically, we use the approach proposed in [72], which delivers all calibration and rectification parameters fully automatically after only a couple of minutes processing. While our cameras are fixed with respect to the vehicle body, flexible arrangements could be dealt with using self-calibration methods [46]. Note that the focal points of all cameras are aligned on the same $x/y-$plane. This is important as it allows us to rectify all cameras jointly. The calibration parameters are:

- $\mathbf{s}^{(i)} \in \mathbb{N}^2$ .... Original image size (1392×512)

- $\mathbf{K}^{(i)} \in \mathbb{R}^{3\times3}$ .... Calibration matrices (unrectified)

- $\mathbf{d}^{(i)} \in \mathbb{R}^5$ .... Distortion coefficients (unrectified)

- $\mathbf{R}^{(i)} \in \mathbb{R}^{3\times3}$ .... Rotation from camera 0 to camera i

- $\mathbf{t}^{(i)} \in \mathbb{R}^{1\times3}$ .... Translation from camera 0 to camera i

- $\mathbf{s}^{(i)}_{rect} \in \mathbb{N}^2$ .... Image size after rectification

- $\mathbf{R}^{(i)}_{rect} \in \mathbb{R}^{3\times3}$ .... Rectifying rotation matrix

- $\mathbf{P}^{(i)}_{rect} \in \mathbb{R}^{3\times4}$ .... Projection matrix after rectification

Here, $i \in \{0, 1, 2, 3\}$ is the camera index, where 0 is the left gray scale, 1 the right gray scale, 2 the left color and 3 the right color camera. The variable definitions are compliant with the OpenCV library [23], which has been used for warping the images. After rectification, only the variables with *rect*-subscripts are relevant. Note that due to the pincushion distortion effect the images have been cropped such that the size of the rectified images is slightly smaller than the original size of 1392×512 Pixels.

The projection of a 3D point in rectified camera coordinates $\mathbf{x} = (x, y, z, 1)^{\mathsf{T}}$ to a point $\mathbf{y} = (u, v, 1)^{\mathsf{T}}$ in the i'th image is given as

$$\mathbf{y} = \mathbf{P}_{rect}^{(i)} \, \mathbf{x} \tag{5.1}$$

with

$$\mathbf{P}_{rect}^{(i)} = \begin{pmatrix} f_u^{(i)} & 0 & c_u^{(i)} & -f_u^{(i)} b_x^{(i)} \\ 0 & f_v^{(i)} & c_v^{(i)} & 0 \\ 0 & 0 & 1 & 0 \end{pmatrix} \tag{5.2}$$

the i'th projection matrix. Here, $b_x^{(i)}$ denotes the baseline (in meters) with respect to reference camera 0. In order to project a 3D point $\mathbf{x}$ in reference camera coordinates to a point $\mathbf{y}$ on the i'th image plane, the rectifying rotation matrix $\mathbf{R}_{cam}^{rect}$ must be considered as well:

$$\mathbf{y} = \mathbf{P}_{rect}^{(i)} \, \mathbf{R}_{cam}^{rect} \, \mathbf{x} \tag{5.3}$$

with $\mathbf{R}_{cam}^{rect} = \mathbf{R}_{rect}^{(0)}$ as camera 0 serves as reference. Here, $\mathbf{R}_{cam}^{rect}$ has been expanded to a 4×4 matrix by appending a fourth zero-row and column and setting $\mathbf{R}_{cam}^{rect}(4, 4) = 1$.

5.2.3. Velodyne and IMU Calibration

The Velodyne laser scanner has been registered with respect to the reference camera coordinate system by initializing the rigid body transformation using the method proposed in [72]. Additionally, we have optimized an error criterion based on the Euclidean distance of 50 manually selected correspondences and a robust measure on the disparity error with respect to the 3 top performing stereo methods in the KITTI stereo benchmark [71]. The optimization has been carried out using Metropolis-Hastings sampling, yielding the rigid

Figure 5.2.: **Illustration of the Dataset.** This figure depicts 18 out of the 113 sequences used for evaluation of the presented method. Note the complexity and diversity in scene layout and appearance.

body transformation $\mathbf{T}_{velo}^{cam}$. A 3D point $\mathbf{x}$ in Velodyne coordinates gets then projected to a point $\mathbf{y}$ in the i'th camera image via

$$\mathbf{y} = \mathbf{P}_{rect}^{(i)} \ \mathbf{R}_{cam}^{rect} \ \mathbf{T}_{velo}^{cam} \ \mathbf{x} \tag{5.4}$$

where $\mathbf{T}_{velo}^{cam}$ denotes the rigid transformation between the laser scanner and the reference camera coordinate system.

For registering the IMU/GPS with respect to the Velodyne laser scanner, we drove an '∞'-loop and registered the point clouds using the Point-to-Plane ICP algorithm. Given two trajectories this problem corresponds to the well-known hand-eye-calibration problem which can be solved using standard tools [99], yielding the rigid body transformation $\mathbf{T}_{imu}^{velo}$. A 3D point $\mathbf{x}$ in IMU/GPS coordinates can then be projected to $\mathbf{y}$ in the i'th image using

$$\mathbf{y} = \mathbf{P}_{rect}^{(i)} \ \mathbf{R}_{cam}^{rect} \ \mathbf{T}_{velo}^{cam} \ \mathbf{T}_{imu}^{velo} \ \mathbf{x} \tag{5.5}$$

Note that the Velodyne sensor only serves as a reference and is not used in our experiments in Chapter 5. However, we have included it here for completeness.

5.3. Data Collection and Annotation

For the experiments conducted in this thesis 113 realistic video sequences have been recorded with a duration of 5 to 30 seconds each, featuring straights, 3-armed and 4-armed intersection scenarios. Each sequence captures the moment of approaching an intersection or waiting in front of a red traffic light. All sequences are manually clipped at the moment the intersection is entered as this is the time when an autonomous system would need to take a decision. Note that this would also be possible in an automatic manner using approximate maps and state-of-the-art localization techniques [29]. Fig. 5.2 depicts a couple of sequences from our dataset. Note

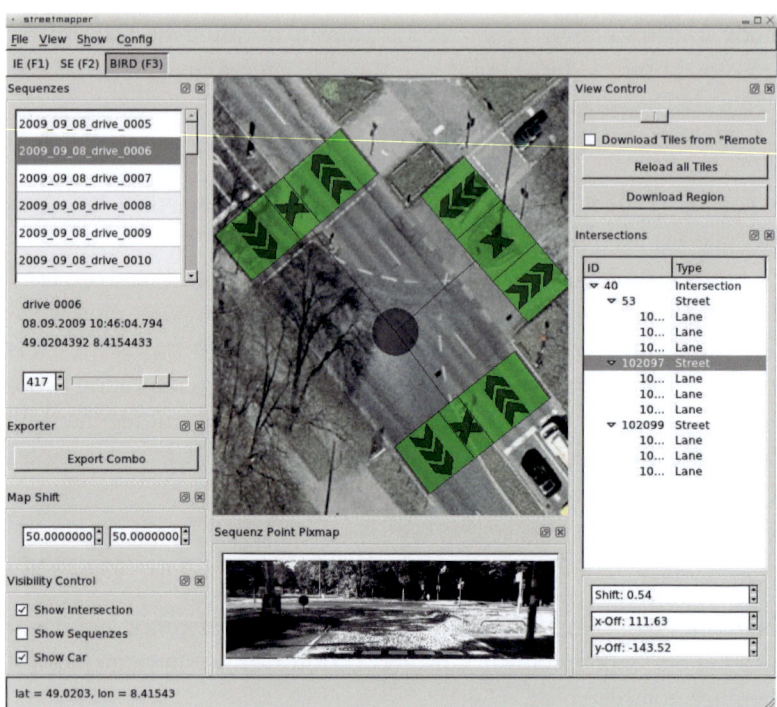

Figure 5.3.: **Intersection Annotation Utility.** The annotation of the 113 sequences with ground truth information has been carried out with an OpenGL tool, that displays image sequences, trajectories, GoogleMaps images and labeled intersections in bird's eye perspective.

the large variability in terms of scene layout and dynamic objects present in the scene.

Annotation of the data has been carried out via GoogleMaps aerial images. For each intersection in the database we labeled the center of the intersection as well as the number, orientation and width of the intersecting streets in bird's eye perspective. A screen shot of our OpenGL annotation tool is shown in Fig. 5.3. Afterwards, the annotated geometry is mapped into the road coordinate system using the GPS coordinates of the vehicle, the road plane estimate and the calibration parameters described in the previous section. Fig. 5.6 shows the variability in terms of road layouts (red) in our dataset.

Additionally, we annotated all vehicle tracklets that have been detected by the approach described in Section 4.1 with the index (l) of the corresponding lane or parking area. For vehicles that have been associated to a lane, the tangent at the closest foot point of lane l is used as object orientation ground truth. Furthermore, we manually annotate all lanes in each scenario with a binary label indicating if the lane is 'active' or not, i.e., if moving vehicles on that lane can be observed or not.

5.4. Experimental Results

Our experiments target at evaluating the overall performance as well as the importance of each individual feature cue for the different tasks, which are detailed in the following sections. Let us define the following feature abbreviations

P = **P**rior (see Section 3.3.1)
T = **T**racklets (see Section 3.3.2)
V = **V**anishing Lines (see Section 3.3.3)
S = **S**emantic labels (see Section 3.3.4)
F = Scene **F**low (see Section 3.3.5)
O = **O**ccupancy Grid (see Section 3.3.6)

which allow for easy indexing of the prior and the feature cues. To gain insights into the strengths and weaknesses of each term in the proposed model, we conduct experiments using the following feature combinations

P .... Prior only
PT, PV, PS, PF, PO .... Single term
PVSFO, PTSFO, PTVFO, PTVSO, PTVSF . All terms but one
PTVSFO .... Full model

i.e., we evaluate the prior without any image cues, the prior in combination with a single feature term, all feature terms but one and the full model including all terms from Section 3.5.2. For each of these settings a separate set of parameters Θ maximizing the respective probability distribution is learned.

5.4.1. Learning the Model Parameters

Due to the relatively small number of sequences in the dataset, we leverage 10-fold cross-validation to evaluate the proposed method: We hold out every 10'th data point (i.e., sequence) for evaluation when training the model parameters Θ using the approach described in Section 3.5.2. Fig. 5.4 and Fig. 5.5 depict the learning curves of the first fold for each feature term combination. For fitting all curves into a single plot, all values have been normalized to the interval $[0, 1]$. In contrast to classical gradient ascent methods, our gradients are noisy due to the non-deterministic nature of the Markov chains that run within the learning procedure. Nevertheless, convergence typically occured after 150-250 gradient ascent steps. During the final iterations of the learning procedure we reduce the learning rate η step-by-step to force all parameters to settle at their final values.

Note that for the prior parameters we slightly deviate from the derivations in Section 3.5.2 and only optimize a scalar precision parameter that we multiply with the maximum-likelihood estimate of the precision matrix. Empirically we found this to perform equally well compared to the full optimization while at the same time being significantly faster and more stable to optimize. Similarly, the mean vector is obtained using maximum-likelihood and kept constant during optimization. Furthermore, we exclude ζ_t, ζ_v and ζ_f from the optimization as these parameters are difficult to optimize and can be easily chosen based on empiric reasoning. All parameters which are not part of Θ and thus not optimized for are summarized in Table 5.1 for reproducibility of the results.

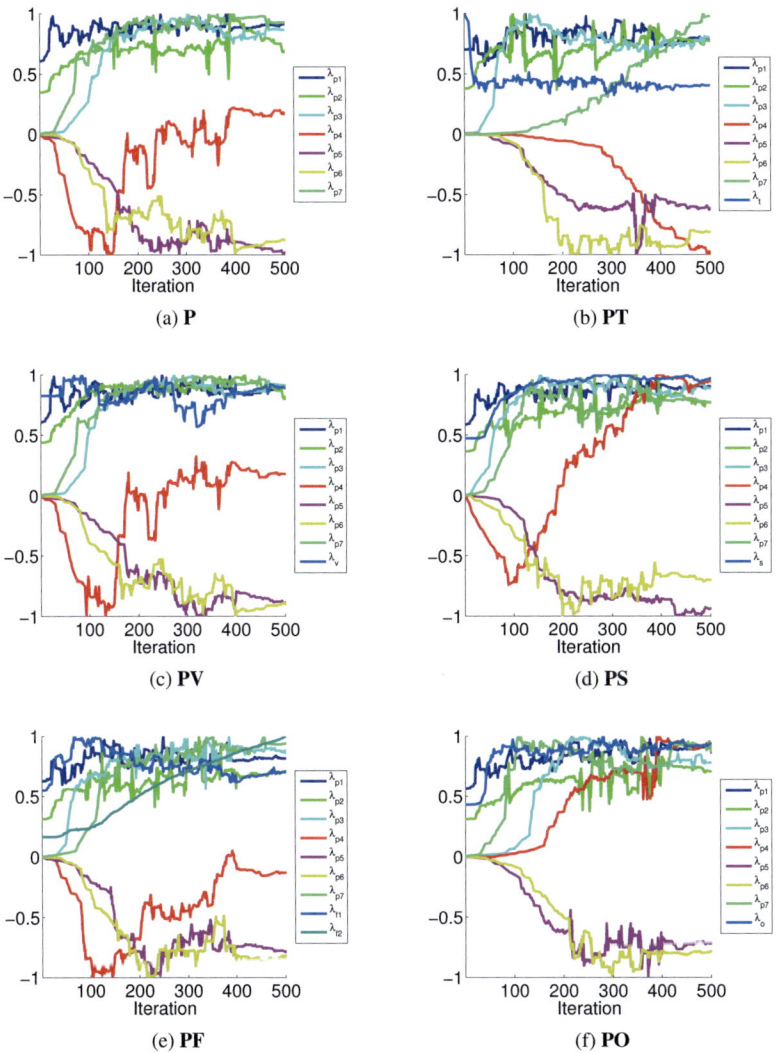

Figure 5.4.: **Learning the Model Parameters.** This figure depicts the evolution of the parameters Θ over the number of gradient ascent steps for each of the settings from Section 5.4.

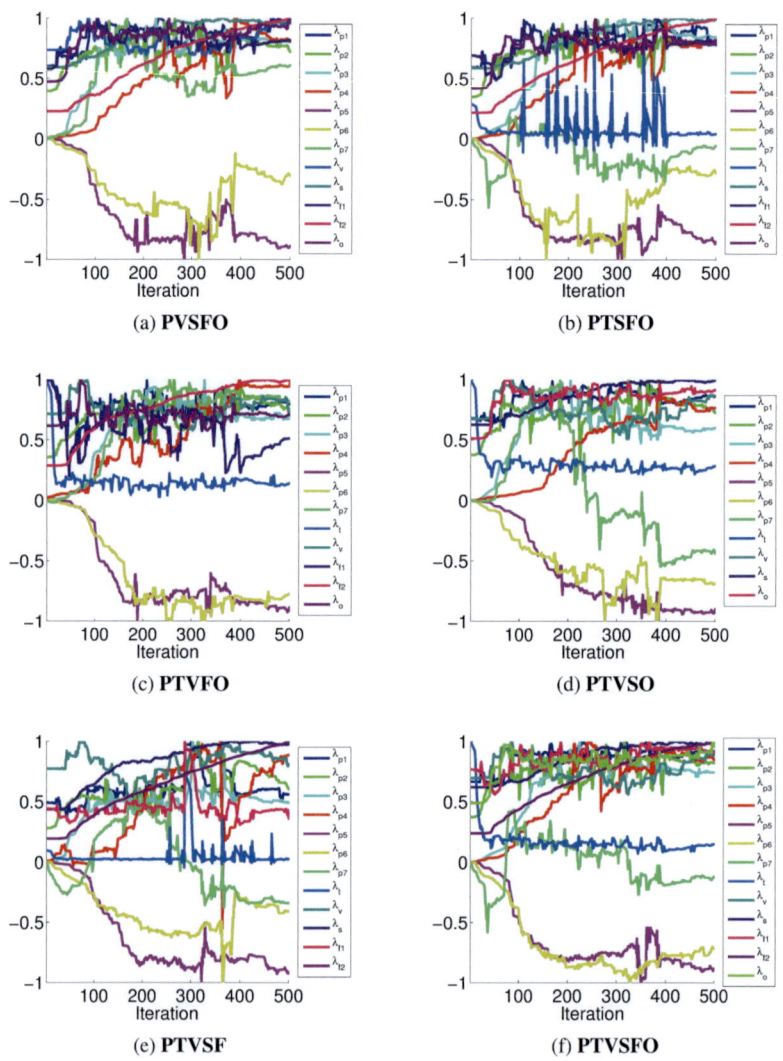

Figure 5.5.: **Learning the Model Parameters.** This figure depicts the evolution of the parameters Θ over the number of gradient ascent steps for each of the settings from Section 5.4.

Prior: (Section 3.3.1)
$\sigma_\alpha = 0.1$ rad   KDE kernel bandwidth

Vehicle Tracklets: (Section 3.3.2 and Section 4.1)
$\tau_d = 0.2$ NMS overlap threshold (object detection)
$\tau_{t1} = 0.5$ Gating threshold (tracking stage 1)
$\tau_{t2} = 0.3$ Gating threshold (tracking stage 2)
$\zeta_t = 10^{-20}$ Outlier threshold
$\sigma_{out} = 70$ m   Std. deviation of outlier distribution

Vanishing Points: (Section 3.3.3)
$\zeta_v = 10^{-10}$ Outlier threshold

Semantic Scene Labels: (Section 3.3.4 and Section 4.3)
$n_s = 4$ Px   Image patch (superpixel) size
$\mathbf{w}_s = (1, 1, 4)$ Scene label weights

Scene Flow: (Section 3.3.5 and Section 4.4)
$n_f = 50$ Number of RANSAC samples
$\zeta_f = 10^{-15}$ Outlier threshold
$\sigma_{out} = 70$ m   Std. deviation of outlier distribution

Occupancy Grid: (Section 3.3.6 and Section 4.5)
$n_o = 1$ m   Occupancy grid cell size
$\mathbf{w}_o = (-1, 4, 1)$ Weights of geometric prior
$\Delta_o = (2, 20)$ m   Margins of geometric prior

Inference and Learning: (Section 3.4 and Section 3.5)
$n_{infer} = 10,000$ Number of samples drawn at inference
$n_{learn} = 10$ Number of samples per learning iteration
$n_{iter} = 500$ Number of learning iterations

Sampling: (Table 3.1)
$\upsilon_c \in \{0.5, 5.0\}$ m   Proposal std. deviation (center)
$\sigma_w \in \{0.5, 5.0\}$ m   Proposal std. deviation (street width)
$\sigma_\alpha \in \{0.02, 0.2\}$ rad   Proposal std. deviation (crossing angle)
$\sigma_r \in \{0.01, 0.1\}$ rad   Proposal std. deviation (rotation)

Table 5.1.: **Constants.** This table shows the setting of all constants in our model. All values have been kept fix throughout all experiments reported in this thesis.

5.4.2. Expressive Power and Generality

To accommodate for the noise in the features and the difficult nature of the estimation problem in general, the proposed geometric model from Section 3.1 is simplified in a sense that it forces opposing streets to be collinear and all streets to share the same width. To justify this approximation and demonstrate the applicability of the proposed intersection model to real-world scenes, we fit the model parameters $\mathcal{R} = \{\kappa, \mathbf{c}, w, r, \alpha\}$ to the true intersection layouts that have been annotated using GoogleMaps images and compare the road area overlap. This leads to an 'oracle' measure of the maximum performance that can be achieved with our model when assuming complete and perfect observations. For each scene, we maximize the overlapping road area using iterative non-linear optimization on the intersection-over-union criterion

$$\hat{\mathcal{R}} = \operatorname*{argmax}_{\mathcal{R}} \underbrace{\frac{\operatorname{road}(\mathcal{R}, \bar{w}) \cap \operatorname{road}(\mathcal{G}, \bar{w})}{\operatorname{road}(\mathcal{R}, \bar{w}) \cup \operatorname{road}(\mathcal{G}, \bar{w})}}_{\text{overlapping road area}} \qquad (5.6)$$

where $\operatorname{road}(\cdot, d)$ is a function that returns the road region clipped at distance d from the intersection center $\mathbf{c}$, $\bar{w}$ is the average street width, $\mathcal{R}$ is the simplified model and $\mathcal{G}$ denotes the ground truth layout.

Fig. 5.6 shows the results of this optimization, ordered by decreasing overlap. The ground truth and the simplified intersection layout are shown in red and blue, respectively. The average overlap on all 113 sequences is 86.9%. Given the fact that preliminary experiments [69, 74] indicate an expected performance between 45% and 60%, and that the street width is often hard to observe or not observable at all (e.g., due to the low camera viewpoint and clutter), the geometric approximations seem justified. For the vast majority of intersection geometries in Fig. 5.6 the simplified model in blue is a good approximation to the full model, illustrated in red, yet it can be described with a significantly smaller amount of parameters. Note that the 113

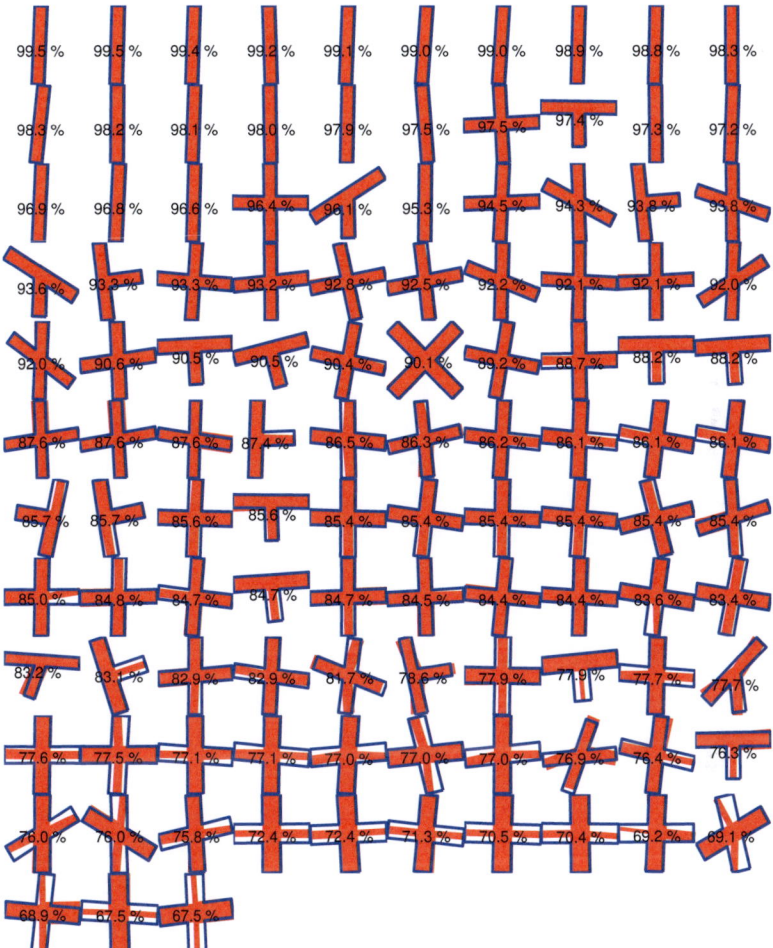

Figure 5.6.: **Expressive Power of the Geometric Model.** This figure illustrates the generality of the restricted geometric model presented in Section 3.1 (blue) with respect to the ground truth road layout (red). All 113 intersections from our dataset are shown, sorted by decreasing overlap. As expected, straight roads can be approximated best, while X-crossings sometimes appear in more esoteric shapes. Overall, the simplified model provides a good approximation to the true intersection layout.

scenarios under consideration are chosen at random from real-world test runs and are representative for the distribution of intersection layouts in Karlsruhe.

5.4.3. Sampling from the Road Layout Prior

To confirm the quality of the learned road layout prior $p(\mathcal{R}; \Theta)$ we draw 120 random samples from it using the parameter set Θ from training fold one. The resulting samples are depicted in Fig. 5.7 using the same axis limits for each subplot. As evidenced by this experiment, the synthesized intersections exhibit different topologies, locations, scales and street orientations. Qualitatively, the samples resemble natural intersections well. The impact of including this prior knowledge into the inference process is evaluated quantitatively in Section 5.4.4. Note that simple left or right turns ($\kappa \in \{2, 3\}$) have not been observed in our dataset which is also reflected by the samples from the prior.

5.4.4. Topology and Geometry

To judge the performance of the proposed model, we evaluate the estimation results of each setting against several metrics. First, we measure the accuracy in topology estimation, which is the percentage of all 113 cases in which the correct topology κ has been recovered. Furthermore, we propose three geometric metrics: We compute the average Euclidean error in estimating the center of the intersection, the average street orientation error and the road area overlap.

Regarding the street orientation, we assign each street to its (rotationally) closest counterpart in the ground truth layout in order to decouple the orientation measure from the estimated topology κ. More precisely, we take the layout with the smaller number of streets and assign all streets to their closest counterparts in the layout with the larger number of streets. Consider for example a three-way intersection that has been recovered as a four-way intersection or vice versa. If all street orientations have been estimated correctly except for the

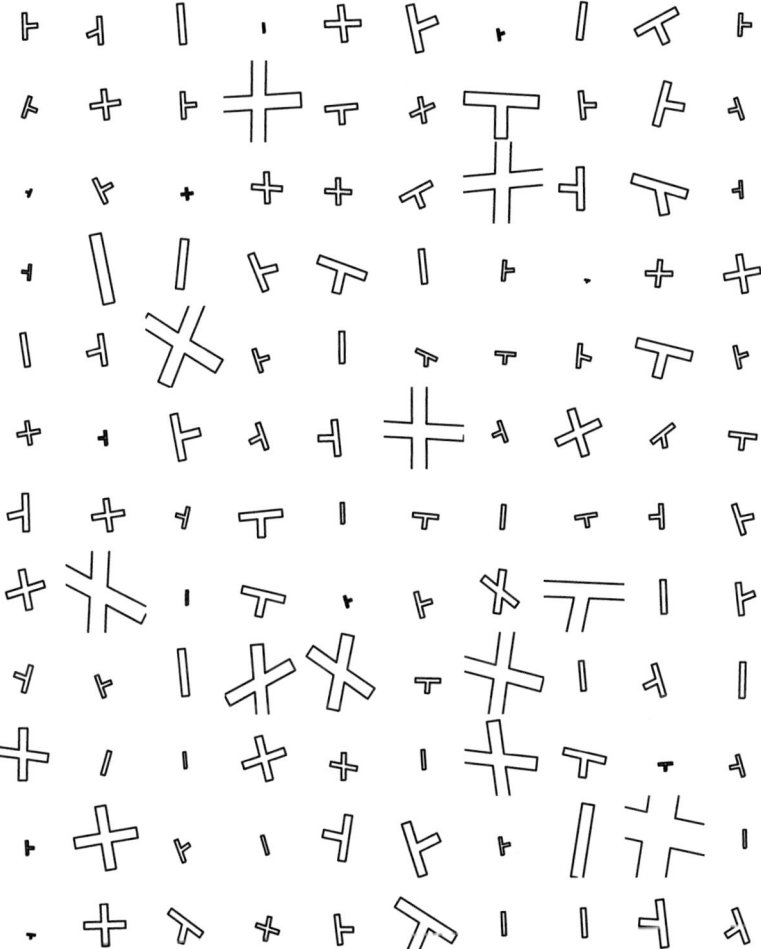

Figure 5.7.: **Samples from the Prior.** This figure shows 120 random samples from the learned prior $p(\mathcal{R})$ in road coordinates ($y = 0$), using the same axis limits in each plot: $x \in [-75, 75]$ and $z \in [-50, 100]$. For clarity, only the left and right road boundaries are shown here.

one that does not exist in the other layout the orientation error is not affected as desired. On contrary, a street that is part of the correct layout but is estimated badly in terms of orientation increases the error.

Finally, the road area overlap measures how much the estimated road layout overlaps with the ground truth layout by computing the intersection-over-union of both road areas. For this evaluation we make use of the measure introduced in Eq. 5.6 in Section 5.4.2. Note that the accuracy is upper bounded by the oracle results depicted in Fig. 5.6 due to the simplified geometric model.

All metrics have been evaluated for each setting and the results are depicted in Table 5.2 (row 1 to 4). The corresponding topology confusion matrices are shown in Fig. 5.8. As evidenced by the experiments, each feature is able to improve the results compared to using prior information alone (column 1-6). The strongest cues in our framework are vehicle tracklets, 3D scene flow and the occupancy grid features. This indicates that despite its noisy nature, depth information is important for solving the problem. The smallest gain in performance is observed for the vanishing point feature. This is because this feature cue only works in combination with other cues as it only allows for 'fine tuning' the street orientations but does not directly influence the existence of a street.

Additional performance gains can be achieved when combining the feature cues. In terms of topology estimation, the best results have been obtained by making us of all information. Without the semantic scene label cue, the geometric error measures can be slightly improved. While these differences are only marginal, our experiments suggest that the semantic scene label cue is the weakest when considered in combination with all the other cues. In contrast, important information is coming from the occupancy grid. Removing this cue significantly impacts the performance, especially in terms of topology and road area estimation, but also regarding the intersection location and street orientation errors. We believe that this is because occupancy information is most complementary to the other cues, while 3D scene flow and vehicle tracklets can partly replace each other.

Note that our learning procedure described in Section 3.5.1 has no access to the metrics we employ here. Instead, it directly maximizes the likelihood of the data with respect to the proposed model. Thus, errors and uncertainties in the ground truth labeling impact performance and explain the differences between the models.

5.4.5. Tracklet Associations and Semantic Activities

Besides the geometric reasoning discussed so far, an important aspect in real-world applications is to understand the scene at a higher level. This includes the association of vehicle tracklets to lanes ('Tracklet Accuracy' in Table 5.2) as well as the detection of active lanes ('Lane Accuracy' in Table 5.2). With active we refer to lanes that have the right of way, i.e., where the green light is turned on in the case of signalized intersections. Note that we are able to infer such information merely by looking at the dynamic objects in the scene. No detection and recognition of traffic lights is required and the state of traffic lights facing towards the other streets are recovered as well.

For evaluating the above mentioned metrics we extract all *unique* tracklets. We define a tracklet as unique if it has a minimum tracklet length of 10 meters and if it has been uniquely assigned to one of the lanes, where uniqueness is measured by the distance of the most likely lane to the second likely in terms of their log-likelihood $\log p(\mathbf{t}|l, \mathcal{R})$ as defined in Eq. 3.12. For all unique tracklets, we evaluate the accuracy in tracklet-to-lane association as well as the accuracy in detecting active lanes. We define a lane as active if at least one tracklet has been uniquely assigned to it. Note that we assign the tracklets to the closest lanes in the ground truth layout to account for the fact that the model topology κ might have been wrongly estimated. This is similar to the street orientation evalu-

	P	PT	PV	PS	PF	PO	PVS FO	PTS FO	PTV FO	PTV SO	PTV SF	PTV SFO
1 Topology Accuracy (%, ↑)	19.5	64.6	20.3	55.8	66.4	83.2	91.1	89.4	91.1	90.3	72.6	**92.0**
2 Location Error (m, ↓)	6.8	5.1	6.7	7.9	4.5	4.0	3.0	2.9	**2.7**	3.1	4.8	3.0
3 Street Orient. Err. (deg, ↓)	8.7	5.4	8.7	7.3	5.2	5.1	3.6	3.6	**3.6**	3.6	4.7	3.6
4 Road Area Overlap (%, ↑)	33.1	51.0	32.9	41.2	53.6	63.4	69.3	69.7	**71.2**	68.9	57.5	69.9
5 Tracklet Accuracy (%, ↑)	28.1	78.7	30.0	35.8	79.2	65.1	80.7	80.3	79.8	77.6	81.6	**82.0**
6 Lane Accuracy (%, ↑)	77.3	90.3	78.0	80.2	**90.5**	85.2	89.7	89.4	89.8	88.3	90.2	89.7
7 Object Orient. Err. (deg, ↓)	53.0	17.7	54.4	45.1	17.5	24.2	**14.0**	15.1	14.9	15.4	15.1	14.3
8 Object Detection AP (%, ↑)	73.6	73.7	73.7	73.1	73.6	74.1	74.1	74.1	**74.2**	74.1	73.7	74.0

P	=	**Prior**
T	=	**T**racklets
V	=	**V**anishing Lines
S	=	**S**emantic labels
F	=	Scene **F**low
O	=	**O**ccupancy Grid

Table 5.2.: **Quantitative Results.** This table shows our inference results quantitatively and compares the different settings described in Section 5.4. The metrics are displayed in the left column, with the measurement unit and the metric order in brackets. Regarding the order, ↑ means higher is better and ↓ means lower is better. All numbers represent averages over all 113 shots used in our evaluation.

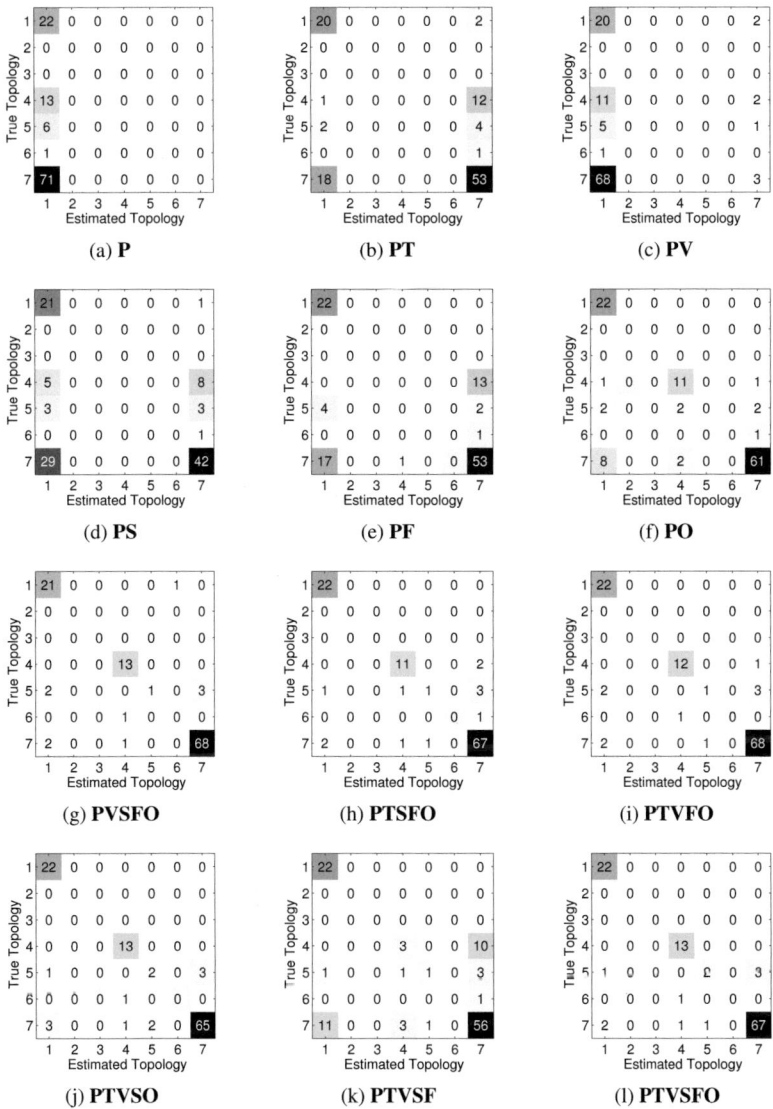

Figure 5.8.: **Topology Confusion Matrices.** This figure depicts the confusion matrices for each setting, with estimated topologies and true topologies at the x- and y-axis, respectively.

ation in the previous section and decouples the error metrics from other parameters.

The tracklet and lane accuracies for all settings are depicted in Table 5.2 (rows 5 and 6). As expected, the best results are obtained in all cases where either the 3D scene flow or the vehicle tracklet features are included in the model, with 80% accuracy in tracklet associations and 90% accuracy in the active lane detection experiment. While the boost in tracklet accuracy performance is dramatic compared to using prior knowledge alone (28% accuracy), lane accuracy increases from 77% to 90%. The reason is that most of the lanes are inactive, hence strongly biasing the dataset. However, note that the improvements by our model still correspond to a relative error reduction of over 50%.

5.4.6. Object Orientation Estimation

The estimated object orientations that serve as input to our tracklet model in Section 3.3.2 are noisy as evidenced by the confusion matrix in Fig. 4.2. In fact, the average orientation error made by the object detector described in the previous section is 32.6 degrees. Using our extracted scene topology, geometry and lane association knowledge, however, we are able to re-estimate the orientations of each object assuming that all vehicles adhere to some basic traffic rules, i.e., right handed traffic. For associating the tracklets to lanes and the detections to lane spline points, we employ the inference procedure described in Section 3.4.2. Next, we select the tangent angle at the associated spline's foot point s on the inferred lane l as our novel orientation estimate. Since parked cars are often oriented arbitrarily, our evaluation focuses on moving vehicles only. Table 5.2 (row 7) shows that we are able to significantly reduce the orientation error from 32.6 degrees, which corresponds to the orientation error of the raw detections (not depicted in the table), down to 14.0 degrees when using our model in combination with vehicle tracklets or 3D scene flow.

5.4.7. Object Detection

As we have shown in Section 5.4.4, objects help in estimating the layout and geometry of the scene. On the other hand, knowledge about the road layout should also help in improving the performance of object detectors. To verify this hypothesis, we conduct the following experiment.

We manually annotated all cars in the last frame of each sequence using 2D bounding boxes. This results in 355 labeled car instances in total. Next, we ran our pre-trained part-based object detector [60] from Section 4.1.1 on those images and apply non-maxima-suppression on the detections. Note that these detections are the same as the ones that serve as input to our tracking model described in Section 3.3.2 and Section 4.1.2. Given the object detections and the inferred road geometry from Section 5.4.4, we re-score each object detection by adding the following term to the scores of [60]

$$0.5 \left[\max_l \, \exp\left(-\frac{\Delta_l^2}{2w^2}\right) + \sum_{i=1}^{3} \exp\left(-\frac{(x_i - \mu_i)^2}{2\sigma_i^2}\right) \right] - 1 \quad (5.7)$$

Here Δ_l is the distance of a car detection to lane spline l, w is the estimated street width and $\{\mu_i, \sigma_i\}$ are mean and standard deviation of the object width, height and position, respectively, obtained from a held-out training set using maximum likelihood estimation. Due to the choice of Eq. 5.7, a value between -1 and $+1$ will be added to the detector score, depending on the agreement in size and the proximity to the closest lane.

Fig. 5.9 depicts the precision-recall curves for the L-SVM baseline [60] and our approach. As evidenced by this figure, our geometric and topological constraints increase detection performance significantly, improving average precision from 69.9% to 74.2%. The benefits of including this knowledge into the detection process are also illustrated in Fig. 5.10. In order to include the partly occluded car to the right into the detection result, the threshold of the baseline has to

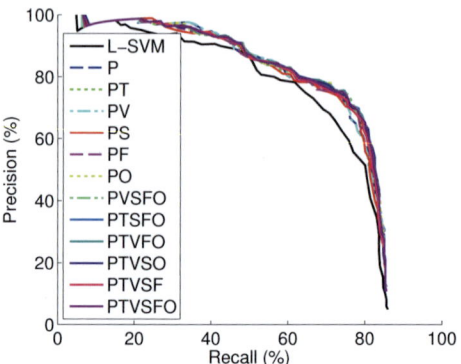

Figure 5.9.: **Improving Object Detection.** This figure shows the precision-recall curves for the object detection task using an overlap threshold of 50%. Compared to Felzenszwalb et al. [60] (L-SVM), context from the proposed model helps to improving object detection performance.

be lowered to a value which produces two false positives (top). In contrast, our re-scored ranking is able to handle this case (bottom). The average precision for each setting is listed in Table 5.2 (row 8).

5.4.8. Runtime

In this section we evaluate the computational complexity of the proposed approach experimentally. Towards this goal, we measure the running times of our mixed MATLAB/C++ implementation. While parts of the algorithm already run in real-time and others can be accelerated using instruction- or thread-level parallelism, this was not the primary goal of this thesis and is left to future work. However, this evaluation provides a good indication of the bottlenecks and the more efficient stages in our implementation.

Table 5.3 lists the average running times of the individual stages of our algorithm, separated into feature extraction (top) and model inference (bottom). Learning times are in the order of hours, depending on the quality of the gradient approximation, but not listed here as learning can be performed offline. On average, our method

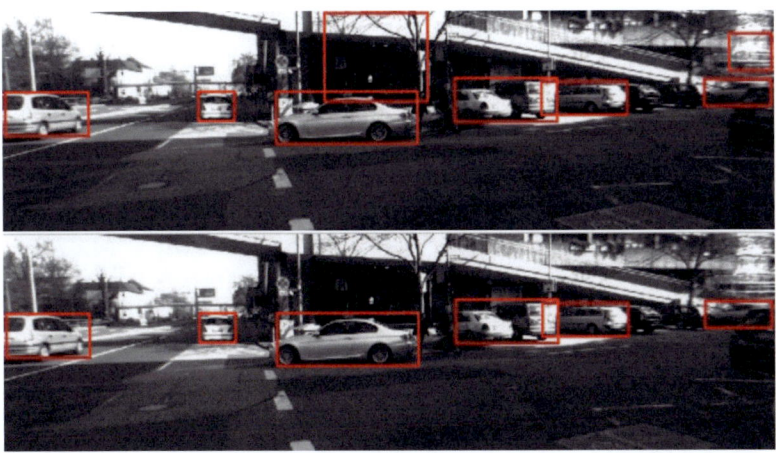

Figure 5.10.: **Improving Object Detection.** By using context from our model for re-weighting object hypothesis our algorithm (bottom) is able to eliminate false positives of state-of-the-art part-based object detectors [60] (top).

runs at ~ 8 seconds per frame, when including the time for feature extraction and drawing $10,000$ samples from the model. While the time for inference could be dramatically reduced when using a pure C++ implementation and parallel Markov chains, the main bottleneck of our method is the feature extraction stage. In particular, the running times are heavily dominated by the time consumed to detect and track objects, even though the cascaded version [61] of the part-based object detector [60] has been leveraged, which reduces object detection runtime by a factor of 10, approximately. With the availability of faster object detectors [53, 19] and heavy multi-processing, a real-time implementation seems within reach.

	Frame	Sequence
Object Detection (Section 4.1.1)	3.88 s	314.01 s
Object Tracking (Section 4.1.2)	0.46 s	37.55 s
Long Line Detection (Section 4.2)	0.03 s	2.14 s
Vanishing Line Estimation (Section 4.2)	0.01 s	0.70 s
Semantic Scene Labels (Section 4.3)	0.01 s	1.01 s
Scene Flow / Egomotion (Section 4.4)	0.31 s	24.87 s
Road Plane Estimation (Section 4.4)	0.06 s	5.13 s
Stereo Matching (Section 4.5)	0.30 s	23.90 s
Occupancy Grid Estimation (Section 4.5)	0.09 s	7.41 s
Prior (Section 3.3.1)	0.12 s	9.85 s
Tracklets (Section 3.3.2)	1.28 s	103.54 s
Vanishing Points (Section 3.3.3)	0.10 s	8.19 s
Semantic Labels (Section 3.3.4)	0.60 s	48.21 s
Scene Flow (Section 3.3.5)	0.50 s	40.22 s
Occupancy Grid (Section 3.3.6)	0.18 s	14.41 s
Total	7.92 s	641.13 s

Table 5.3.: **Running Times per Frame/Sequence on a Intel Core7@2.67 Ghz.** This figure shows the average running times of the individual parts of our algorithm on a single CPU core using a mixed MATLAB/C++ implementation. The first part of the table lists the time used for computing the image evidence (feature extraction) and the second part shows the timings for evaluating $10,000$ samples. On average, our basic implementation runs at ~ 8 seconds per frame.

5.4.9. Qualitative Results

Fig. 5.11-5.13 illustrate our inference results for the setting 'PTVSFO', with the most likely lanes for each unique tracklet, indicated by an arrow. The ego-vehicle (observer) is depicted in black. For a definition of uniqueness, the reader is referred to Section 5.4.5.

For most sequences the road layout has been estimated correctly and the vehicles have been assigned to the correct lanes. Only vehicles that are very far away or visible only for a couple of frames pose problems in terms of their lane associations. However, note that this didn't affect the layout estimation. In Fig. 5.11 (top-left) the moving vehicle in front of the observer and the static vehicles at the side of the road have been identified correctly. In Fig. 5.11 (bottom-left) the cyan object has been observed only for a short period of time, leading to a probability of moving forward as well as making a right turn. In Fig. 5.11 (bottom-right) the two crossing vehicles have been identified correctly and distinguished from the vehicles waiting in front of the traffic light. However, the red car has been assigned to the wrong lane as the object detector orientation estimate was too uncertain and no motion has been observed. The same holds true for the red vehicle in Fig. 5.12 (top-left), which has been detected only for a very short period of time.

Typical failure modes are depicted in Fig. 5.14. In Fig. 5.14 (top-left, top-right, bottom-right) the wrong intersection layout has been recovered. However, note that given the estimated layout, most of the lane associations are correct. Fig. 5.14 (middle-right) is a difficult case as no moving vehicles were present to support the hypothesis of a third intersection arm, resulting in a straight road. While the street width has been wrongly estimated in Fig. 5.14 (bottom-left), the layout is correct and almost all vehicles have been associated with the right lanes. In summary, the proposed system works well and robustly. Furthermore, even in the rare event of topology or geometry estimation failures many objects are still correctly inferred.

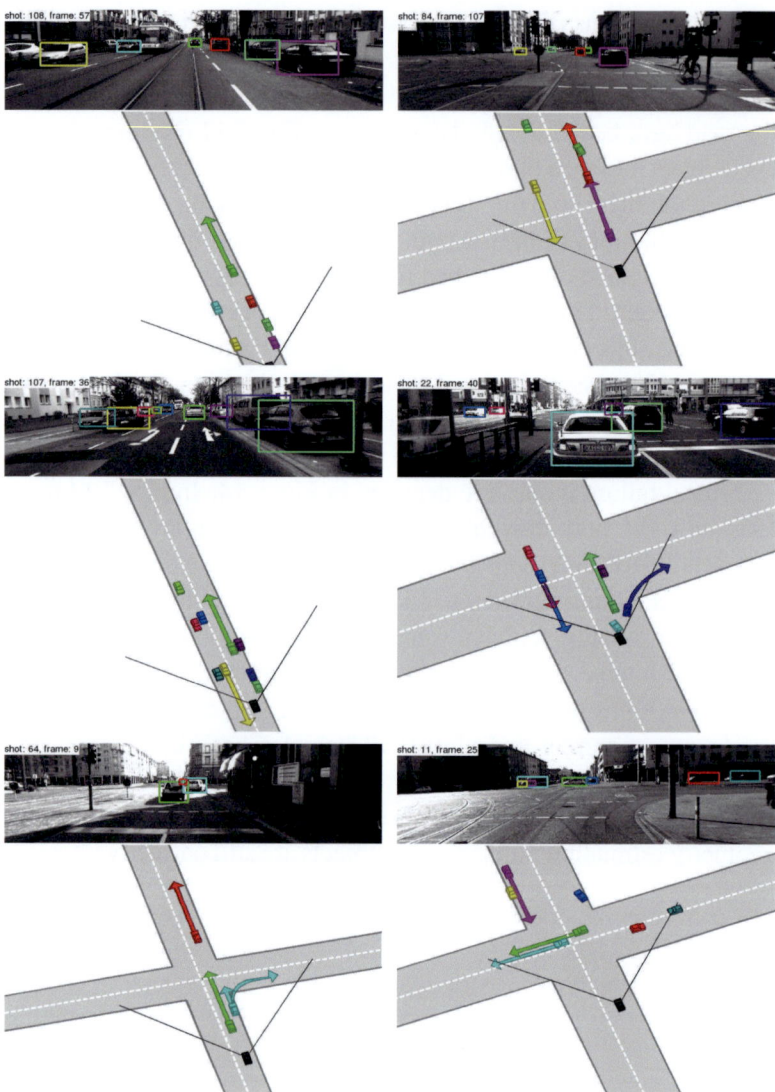

Figure 5.11.: **Inference Results.** For each sequence, the top plot shows the input image with the bounding boxes of the detected objects. The bottom plot shows the inference result from bird's eye perspective. Arrows indicate the predicted driving direction(s).

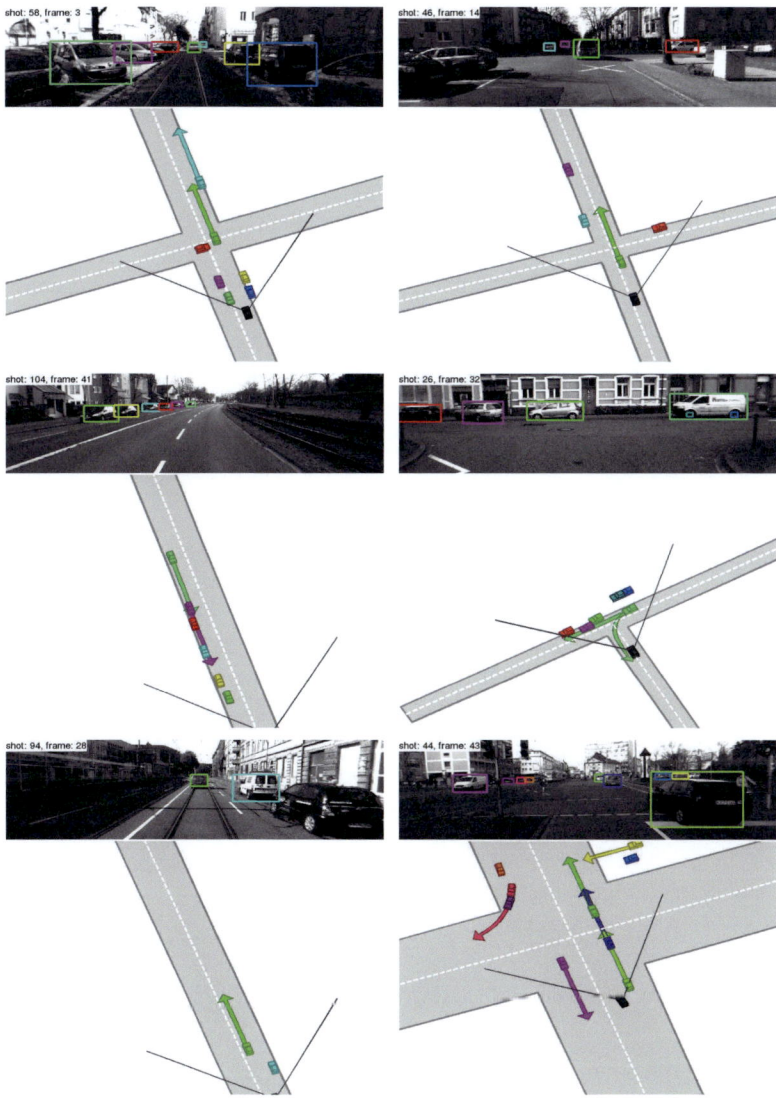

Figure 5.12.: **Inference Results.** For each sequence, the top plot shows the input image with the bounding boxes of the detected objects. The bottom plot shows the inference result from bird's eye perspective. Arrows indicate the predicted driving direction(s).

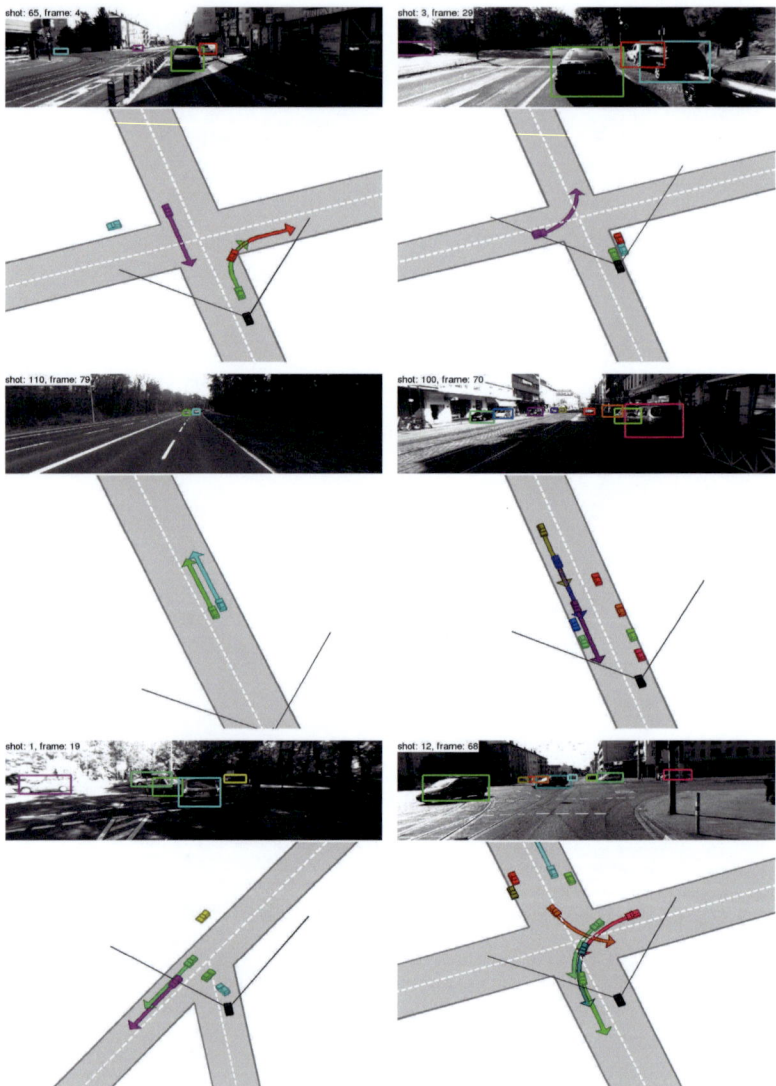

Figure 5.13.: **Inference Results.** For each sequence, the top plot shows the input image with the bounding boxes of the detected objects. The bottom plot shows the inference result from bird's eye perspective. Arrows indicate the predicted driving direction(s).

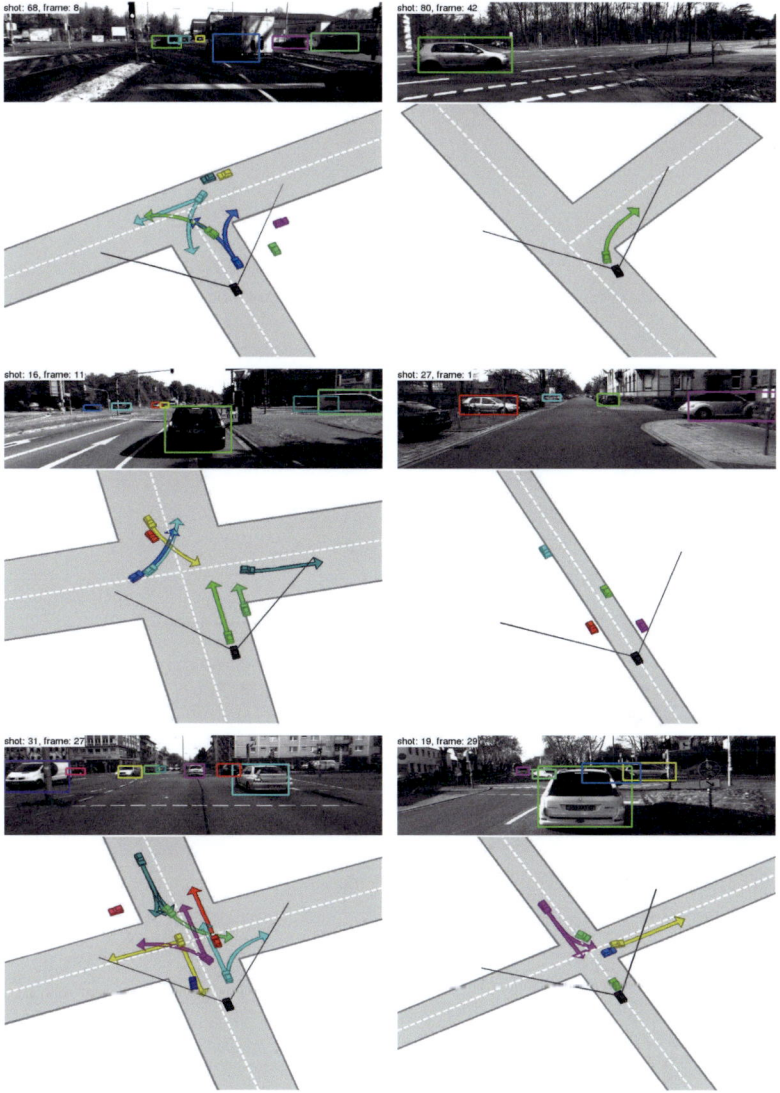

Figure 5.14.: **Failure Cases.** This figure shows some failure modes of our algorithm, where either the topology, geometry or the tracklet associations are (partly) wrong. Section 5.4.9 gives further details.

6. Conclusions and Future Directions

This thesis has proposed a probabilistic generative model, which is able to reason about complex inner-city traffic scenes using features extracted from short (stereo) video sequences recorded from a movable platform. The application is autonomous driving, which currently cannot handle urban environments due to missing or corrupt GPS information, outdated maps, the complexity of the scenes, the amount of clutter (e.g., shadows, vegetation) as well as the high level of occlusions (e.g., occlusions caused by cars, buildings, vegetation or infrastructure). Simple extensions of state-of-the-art lane detectors or lane-keeping systems to intersections are doomed to fail as lane markings are often missing, damaged or occluded.

To provide an alternative, here we have proposed a probabilistic model and image likelihoods using five complementary feature cues that consider the scene as a whole: Vehicle tracklets, vanishing points, semantic labels, 3D scene flow and occupancy grids. By making use of these cues our model is able to extract information such as the topology and geometry of the road layout, as well as the lanes on which vehicles are driving. We have shown that, despite the fact that the partition function of the probabilistic model is intractable to compute, parameter learning is still possible in our model. We have cast the problem as a Gibbs random field and apply contrastive divergence in combination with Markov Chain Monte Carlo inference techniques.

The validity of the proposed model has been substantiated by comprehensive experiments, considering individual image cues as well as a large variety of combinations. On a set of 113 realistic real-world intersection sequences we are able to estimate the topology of the scene with an accuracy of up to 90% while at the same time accurately determining the intersection center and the individual street orientations. Vice-versa, we have shown that context from our model helps in improving the performance of state-of-the-art object detectors in terms of detecting objects as well as estimating their orientation. Considering the scene as a whole turned out to be crucial, especially in the presence of clutter and missing data.

While we have discovered that all features proposed in this work were able to improve performance individually, occupancy grids as well as vehicle tracklets and 3D scene flow have been identified as the strongest and most important feature cues. This is comprehensible as human drivers likewise examine other traffic participants as well as the 3D structure (e.g., buildings, urban canyons) to picture the scene.

Regarding future extensions, models that incorporate typical traffic patterns and traffic light phases will present an interesting area of research. Presently, noise in the observations can lead to implausible configurations such as cars colliding with each other. Including higher-level information such as traffic patterns and traffic light phases will help to reduce ambiguities and increase robustness. Such information will also allow for the detection of abnormalities in the traffic flow and to warn the driver before entering the intersection.

Furthermore, more complex vehicle motion models are required. The presented model uses a simple forward motion constraint with a B-spline based lane model. Improved sensor observations and more computing power will allow for more accurate motion models and lane representations. Another interesting direction will be to integrate information from other traffic participants (e.g., pedestrians) into the model as well as to make use of further sources of information such as road markings whenever they are visible and reliable or street maps, e.g., OpenStreetMap. While maps can be noisy or even outdated, they still provide valuable prior information and can be updated in an online manner as soon as enough vehicles have been equipped with a scene understanding system like the one proposed in this thesis.

A. Sampling Techniques

This appendix gives an introduction to sampling techniques, in particular Markov Chain Monte Carlo (MCMC) methods [5, 123], which are adopted for inference in the scene understanding model presented in this thesis. The robot localization examples used for illustration are gratefully borrowed from a tutorial presentation of Martin Lauer in 2010 [123].

A.1. Introduction

Many statistical problems of practical relevance lead to problems which include solving an integral that is analytically intractable. In Bayesian inference, for example, one is typically interested in inferring unknown variables x from observed data y, which leads to the following problems:

- Normalization: $p(x|y) = \frac{p(y|x)p(x)}{\int p(y|x')p(x')dx'}$

- Marginalization: $p(x|y) = \int p(x,z|y)dz$

- Expectation: $E_p(f(x)) = \int f(x)p(x)dx$

Examples for the latter are:

- The expectation: $\int xp(x)dx$,

- The variance: $\int x^2 p(x)dx - \left(\int xp(x)dx\right)^2$, or

- The expected risk: $\int \text{risk}(x)p(x)dx$

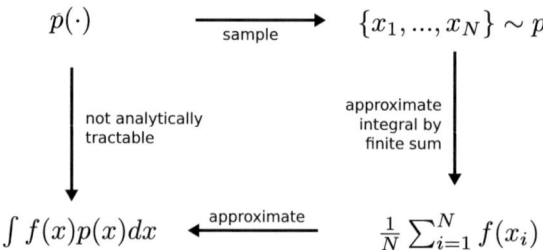

Figure A.1.: **Monte Carlo Approximation** of an integral with a finite sum.

Unfortunately, these integrals are often analytically intractable and sometimes p can not even be expressed as a function. An approximation scheme for solving these tasks is random Monte Carlo simulations, in which the integral

$$\int f(x)p(x)dx \tag{A.1}$$

is approximated by a finite sum

$$\frac{1}{N}\sum_i f(x_i) \tag{A.2}$$

where x_i are samples drawn from p. The longer we run the Monte Carlo simulation, the better the approximation of the integral:

$$\frac{1}{N}\sum_{i=1}^{N} f(x_i) \xrightarrow{N\to\infty} \int f(x)p(x)dx \tag{A.3}$$

Thus the estimate is unbiased and will almost surely converge to the right value by the strong law of large numbers. The Monte Carlo approximation principle is illustrated in Fig. A.1. Maintaining efficiency is one of the main challenges of Monte Carlo methods.

A.2. Basic Sampling Strategies

Before moving on to Markov chains [5], we will review a set of basic sampling algorithms and illustrate them on simple toy cases.

A.2.1. Inverse Transform Sampling

Assuming we are provided with a random number generator, one can draw samples from distributions for which the cumulative probability distribution is invertible. When this is not the case, one can still draw samples by approximating the inverted cumulative probability distribution using interpolation.

More formally, let us consider a one-dimensional random variable x with probability distribution $p(x)$ from which we want to sample. Let us further assume a uniformly distributed random variable $y \sim \mathcal{U}(0, 1)$ and a function $f(y)$, such that $x = f(y)$. Since probability mass in any differential area must be invariant under change of variables $|p(x)dx| = |p(y)dy|$, the distribution of x will be governed by

$$p(x) = p(y) \left| \frac{dy}{dx} \right| = \left| \frac{dy}{dx} \right|. \tag{A.4}$$

By integration we obtain the cumulative density function (CDF)

$$h(x) \equiv \int_{-\infty}^{x} p(x')dx' = y \tag{A.5}$$

with $x = f(y) = h^{-1}(y)$. This means that to obtain a sample from x we can sample $y \sim \mathcal{U}(0, 1)$ and transform it using the inverse of the integral of the target distribution $p(x)$. To illustrate this fact we sample from an exponential distribution by sampling from a uniform distribution using this method. Consider

$$p(x) = \begin{cases} \exp(-x) & 0 \leq x, \\ 0 & \text{else} \end{cases} \tag{A.6}$$

115

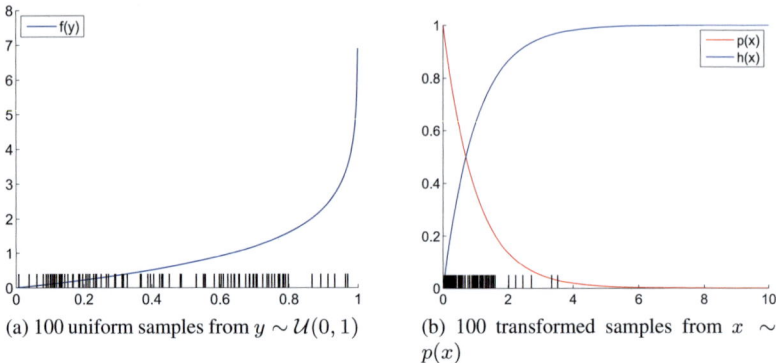

(a) 100 uniform samples from $y \sim \mathcal{U}(0, 1)$

(b) 100 transformed samples from $x \sim p(x)$

Figure A.2.: **Inverse Transform Sampling**. This figure illustrates sampling from a distribution $p(x)$ with invertible CDF by uniformly drawing samples on the interval $(0, 1)$ and transforming them by the inverse of the CDF.

which gives $h(x) = 1 - \exp(-x)$. The inverse mapping is given by $f(y) = h^{-1}(y) = -\ln(1-y)$. This is illustrated in Fig. A.2, which shows 100 samples drawn from the distribution Eq. A.6.

A.2.2. Rejection Sampling

Unfortunately, for many distributions the inverse transform sampling procedure is impractical due to their complex form or high dimensionality. An alternative is rejection sampling, which can be applied whenever another proposal distribution $q(x)$ satisfying

$$p(x) \leq Mq(x) \ \text{ with } \ M < \infty \tag{A.7}$$

is available from which samples are obtained more easily and $p(x)$ can be evaluated up to some normalizing constant as illustrated in Fig. A.3. Each sample from the rejection sampler involves generating two random numbers and an accept/reject step:

- Draw a sample x from $p(x)$.

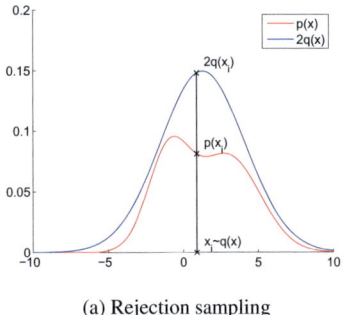

(a) Rejection sampling

Figure A.3.: **Rejection Sampling.** This figure illustrates the target distribution p and the proposal distribution q, satisfying the requirement $p(x) \leq 2q(x)$.

- Draw a sample u from $\mathcal{U}(0, Mq(x))$

If $u \leq p(x)$ the sample is accepted, otherwise it gets rejected. As all accepted samples (x, u) follow a uniform distribution under the curve of $p(x)$ the corresponding x-values are distributed according to $p(x)$ as desired:

$$p(x) \propto q(x) \frac{p(x)}{Mq(x)} \tag{A.8}$$

The procedure is illustrated in Algorithm 4. In practice it is often difficult to bound $p(x)$ by $Mq(x)$. If M is chosen too conservatively (too large) the acceptance probability

$$\Pr(\text{x accepted}) = \Pr\left(u < \frac{p(x)}{Mq(x)}\right) \approx \frac{1}{M} \tag{A.9}$$

gets too small to accept enough samples within reasonable time. This makes rejection sampling impractical in high dimensions.

Let us now consider a simple example. Given independent samples from a Gaussian distribution $\mathcal{N}(0, 0.5)$, we wish to estimate the mean μ and standard deviation σ using rejection sampling. The graphical model is shown in Fig. A.4(a). We draw 50 samples x_i

---

Algorithm 4 Rejection Sampling

$i \leftarrow 1$
while $i < N$ **do**
    draw sample $x_i \sim q(x)$
    draw sample $u_i \sim \mathcal{U}(0,1)$
    if $u_i < \frac{p(x_i)}{Mq(x_i)}$ **then**
        accept x_i
        $i \leftarrow i + 1$

---

from $\mathcal{N}(\mu, \sigma)$ and assume $\mu \sim \mathcal{U}(-0.5, 0.5)$ and $\sigma \sim \mathcal{U}(0.1, 1.1)$ as prior distributions (Fig. A.4(b)). The posterior simplifies to

$$p(\mu, \sigma | x_1, ..., x_N) \propto p(\mu, \sigma)p(x_1, ..., x_N | \mu, \sigma)$$

$$= p(\mu)p(\sigma) \prod_{i=1}^{N} p(x_i | \mu, \sigma)$$

$$= [-0.5 \leq \mu \leq 0.5] \times [0.1 \leq \sigma \leq 1.1]$$

$$\times \left(\frac{1}{\sqrt{2\pi\sigma^2}} \right)^N \exp \left(-\frac{1}{2\sigma^2} \sum_{i=1}^{N} (x_i - \mu)^2 \right)$$

Unfortunately, a tight bound to this density is hard to derive analytically. Hence, we set $q(\mu, \sigma) = p(0, 0.5, | x_1, ..., x_N)$ to be constant. This highlights the main problem with rejection sampling: Finding a tight bound to make sampling tractable. The results of sampling from this posterior are illustrated and compared against the true posterior in Fig. A.4(c)-A.4(e).

Let us now consider a second example which is illustrated in Fig. A.5. Assume, we have a robot which is located in a 2D field of size 1×1 meters, equipped with sensors that measure its distance d_i with respect to the four corners $\mathbf{e}_i$ of the field. We assume a uniform prior for the robot location $\mathbf{x} \sim \mathcal{U}([0,1] \times [0,1])$ and the measurements are given by the robot's position and Gaussian noise $d_i | \mathbf{x} \sim \mathcal{N}(\|\mathbf{x} - \mathbf{e}_i\|, \sigma^2)$ Since all measurements are assumed to

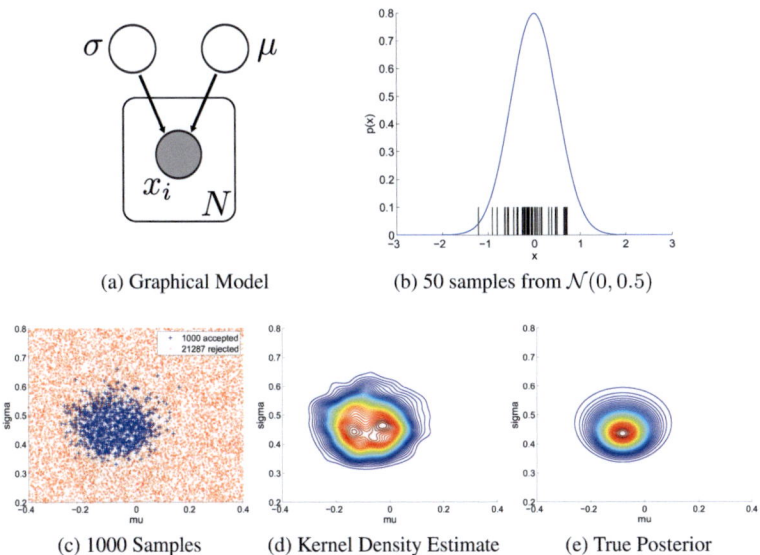

(a) Graphical Model　　　(b) 50 samples from $\mathcal{N}(0, 0.5)$

(c) 1000 Samples　　(d) Kernel Density Estimate　　(e) True Posterior

Figure A.4.: **Rejection Sampling.** Given $N = 50$ independent samples from a Gaussian distribution $\mathcal{N}(\mu, \sigma)$ we infer the posterior over μ and σ.

be independent, the posterior of the robot's position $\mathbf{x}$ given the 4 measurements $\{d_1, ..., d_4\}$ can be written as

$$p(\mathbf{x}|d_1, d_2, d_3, d_4) \ \propto \ p(\mathbf{x})p(d_1|\mathbf{x})p(d_2|\mathbf{x})p(d_3|\mathbf{x})p(d_4|\mathbf{x})$$
$$\propto \ [0 \le x_1, x_2 \le 1]$$
$$\times \exp\left(-\frac{1}{2\sigma^2}\sum_{i=1}^{4}[\|\mathbf{x} - \mathbf{e}_i\| - d_i]^2\right)$$

Since we know that the maximum of the unnormalized posterior is 1, we set $q(\mathbf{x}) = [0 \le x_1, x_2 \le 1]$ which tightly bounds $Zp(x)$, where Z is the normalizing constant. The sampling results are depicted in Fig. A.5(c) and Fig. A.5(d). Note how many rejected samples are required for accepting 50 samples in total.

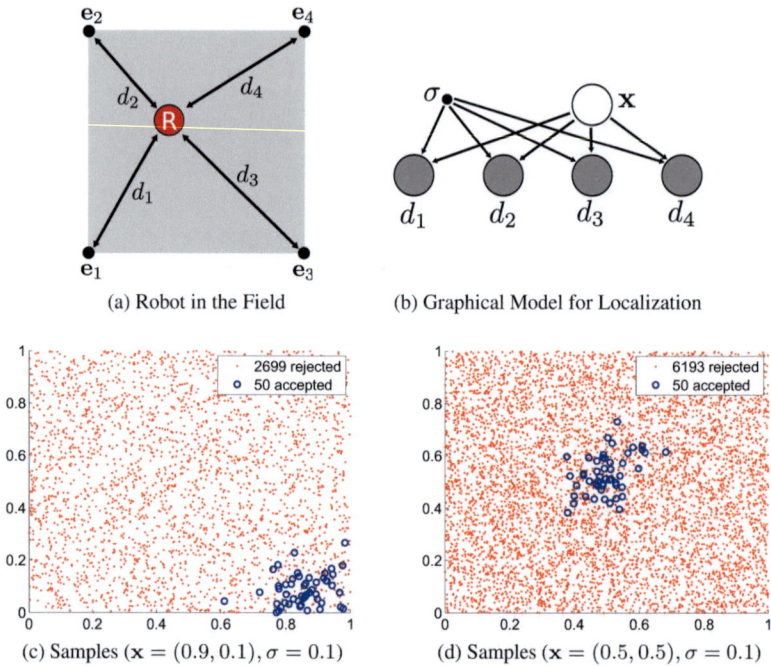

(a) Robot in the Field   (b) Graphical Model for Localization

(c) Samples ($\mathbf{x} = (0.9, 0.1)$, $\sigma = 0.1$)   (d) Samples ($\mathbf{x} = (0.5, 0.5)$, $\sigma = 0.1$)

Figure A.5.: **Robot Localization using Rejection Sampling.** Illustration of the robot localization example: The task is to infer the robot's location given noisy measurements of its distances to the field corners. The lower plots show samples drawn using rejection sampling.

A.3. Markov Chains

While the methods discussed so far are simple, they can be only applied to very simple low-dimensional problems. As a step towards the much more powerful Markov Chain Monte Carlo methods, this section first introduces Markov chains and their properties.

A.3.1. Definition of Markov Chains

Let us start with the definition of Markov chains.

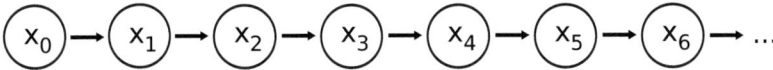

Figure A.6.: **Markov chain.** Each state depends only on its predecessor.

Definition 1 (Markov Chain). *A Markov chain (named after Andrey Markov) is a discrete random process with the Markov property.*

Definition 2 (Random Process). *Let $(\Omega, \mathcal{F}, P)$ be a probability space, with sample space Ω, σ-field $\mathcal{F} \subseteq 2^{\Omega}$ and probability measure $P : \mathcal{F} \to [0, 1]$. Let further $(\Psi, \mathcal{X})$ be a measurable observation space. A random process is a collection of Ψ-valued random variables on Ω:*

$$X = \{x_i : i \in \{1, ..., N\} \wedge x_i : \Omega \to \Psi\}$$

Definition 3 (Markov Property). *A random process is said to be Markov, iff the conditional probability distribution of successor states in the process depends only upon the present state:*

$$P(x_i|x_{i-1}, ..., x_1) = P(x_i|x_{i-1})$$

This simplifies the joint distribution of X to:

$$P(x_1, ..., x_N) = P(x_1) \prod_{i=2}^{N} P(x_i|x_{i-1})$$

The Markov property is illustrated in Fig. A.6, where each variable of the process depends only on the previous variable. An example of a Markov process is the random walk where, at each step, the new position only depends upon the current position. If dynamics is introduced, for example in form of a continuous velocity assumption, the process is no longer Markov, since the new position depends on the current *and* the previous position. However, increasing the dimen-

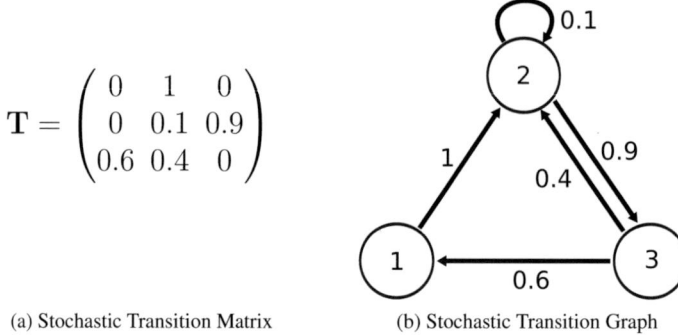

$$T = \begin{pmatrix} 0 & 1 & 0 \\ 0 & 0.1 & 0.9 \\ 0.6 & 0.4 & 0 \end{pmatrix}$$

(a) Stochastic Transition Matrix   (b) Stochastic Transition Graph

Figure A.7.: **Homogeneous Discrete Markov Chain.** This figure shows the stochastic transition matrix and the transition graph of a Markov chain with 3 states. In (a), the ij-th entry of T denotes the probability of transitioning from i to j. (b) shows the corresponding graph.

sionality of the state to two (position, velocity) restores the Markov property again.

A Markov chain for which the transition operator does not depend on time is called *homogeneous* Markov chain. It is convenient to describe homogeneous Markov chains via stochastic transition matrices and directed graphs. This is illustrated in Fig. A.7. Here, transition probabilities are represented as entries in the transition matrix T or labels in the transition graph. Probabilities must be positive and sum to one. The probability distribution for the new state p_i is obtained by multiplying the previous probability vector p_{i-1} by the transition matrix T:

$$\mathbf{p}_i^{\mathsf{T}} = \mathbf{p}_{i-1}^{\mathsf{T}} \mathbf{T} \tag{A.10}$$

Note that we will use $\mathbf{p} = (p(x = s_1), ..., p(x = s_m))^{\mathsf{T}}$ for distributions and p for probabilities, or elements of $\mathbf{p}$. To ensure that probabilities sum to one ($\sum_i \tilde{p}_i = 1$), all rows of T must sum to one. This can be easily verified by rewriting the transition in terms of sums:

$$\tilde{p}_j = \sum_i p_i T_{ij} \tag{A.11}$$

Because of $\sum_j \tilde{p}_j = 1$ we have $\sum_j \sum_i p_i T_{ij} = \sum_i p_i \sum_j T_{ij} = 1$ and since $\sum_i p_i = 1$, it is sufficient that all rows of $\mathbf{T}$ sum to one ($\sum_j T_{ij} = 1$) to ensure valid distributions. In the following we illustrate some iterations of a Markov process. Let's consider the transition matrix

$$\mathbf{T} = \begin{pmatrix} 0.5 & 0 & 0.5 \\ 0.5 & 0.5 & 0 \\ 0 & 0.5 & 0.5 \end{pmatrix} \tag{A.12}$$

and start with $\mathbf{p}_1 = (1, 0, 0)^\mathsf{T}$, a distribution which has all it's probability at state 1. By iterating $\mathbf{p}_i^\mathsf{T} \leftarrow \mathbf{p}_{i-1}^\mathsf{T}\mathbf{T}$, we get:

Iteration i	$\mathbf{p}_i^\mathsf{T}$
1	$(1.00, 0.00, 0.00)$
2	$(0.50, 0.00, 0.50)$
3	$(0.25, 0.25, 0.50)$
4	$(0.25, 0.38, 0.38)$
5	$(0.31, 0.38, 0.32)$
6	$(0.34, 0.34, 0.32)$
7	$(0.33, 0.33, 0.33)$
$\vdots$	$\vdots$
∞	$(0.33, 0.33, 0.33)$

This example already exhibits a desired property of Markov chains: After several iterations the chain stabilizes at a fix point. It is said to be stationary at $\mathbf{p}_\infty = (0.33, 0.33, 0.33)^\mathsf{T}$. For this $\mathbf{T}$, no matter what initial distribution $\mathbf{p}_1$ we use, the chain will always converge to the same stationary point. Note that the stationary point can be computed directly from the stochastic transition matrix $\mathbf{T}$. Since for $\mathbf{p}_\infty$ we have $\mathbf{p}_\infty^\mathsf{T} = \mathbf{p}_\infty^\mathsf{T}\mathbf{T}$, $\mathbf{p}_\infty$ is the left eigenvector of $\mathbf{T}$ corresponding to eigenvalue 1. In the following we will examine sufficient conditions which guarantee convergence of Markov chains.

A.3.2. Properties of Markov Chains

Definition 4 (Stationarity). *A probability distribution* $\mathbf{p}$ *on a state space of a Markov chain with transition matrix* $\mathbf{T}$ *is called stationary, if*

$$\mathbf{p}^\mathsf{T} = \mathbf{p}^\mathsf{T}\mathbf{T}.$$

or in, other words, the probability of being in state x' *is invariant*

$$p(x') = \sum_x p(x)T_{xx'}$$

for any possible state x'. *For the continuous case, the matrix* $\mathbf{T}$ *is replaced by a transition kernel* $T(x'|x)$ *which models the transition probabilities. Thus stationary distributions are those, for which*

$$p(x') = \int p(x)T(x'|x)dx$$

holds.

A stochastic transition matrix $\mathbf{T}$, for which any Markov chain converges to the invariant distribution $p(x)$ is called ergodic. An ergodic Markov chain has exactly one stationary distribution.

Definition 5 (Ergodicity). *Let* $\mathbf{T}_\infty = \lim_{k\to\infty} \mathbf{T}^k$. *A Markov chain with transition matrix* $\mathbf{T}$ *is called ergodic, if*

- $\mathbf{T}_\infty$ *exists*

- *All entries of* $\mathbf{T}_\infty$ *are positive*

- *All rows of* $\mathbf{T}_\infty$ *are identical*

A Markov chain is ergodic, iff it is irreducible and aperiodic.

Definition 6 (Irreducibility). *A Markov chain is called irreducible, if any state* x' *of the chain can be reached by any other state* x *in a finite number of steps. More formally, there must be a sequence* *of states* $(x = x_1, ..., x_N = x')$ *such that* $T_{x_{i-1}x_i} > 0$ *for all* $i \in \{1, ..., N-1\}$.

Through proper state assignment or via permutation using an appropriate permutation matrix $\mathbf{Q}$, the transition matrix $\mathbf{T}$ of a reducible Markov chain can be partitioned into the canonic form

$$\mathbf{QTQ}^{\mathsf{T}} = \begin{pmatrix} \mathbf{C} & \mathbf{A} \\ \mathbf{0} & \mathbf{T} \end{pmatrix} \tag{A.13}$$

with square stochastic matrix $\mathbf{C}$, rectangular non-negative matrix $\mathbf{A}$ and square sub-stochastic matrix $\mathbf{T}$. The states of the Markov chain are partitioned into closed states belonging exclusively to $\mathbf{C}$ and transient states belonging to $\mathbf{T}$. Once a transition into a closed state has been performed, transient states are never reachable again. The eigenvectors of $\mathbf{C}$ define the behavior of the Markov chain at equilibrium.

Definition 7 (Aperiodicity). *A Markov chain is called aperiodic, if the occurrence of states is not restricted to periodic events, but any state may occur at any time. More formally, we define the period of state x as[1]*

$$d_x = gcd \left\{ n \mid \exists(x = x_1, ..., x_n = x) \wedge \forall_{i \in \{2,..,n\}} : T_{x_{i-1}x_i} > 0 \right\}$$

A Markov chain is aperiodic, if all states x have period $d_x = 1$.

If a Markov chain is aperiodic, returns to state x can occur at *irregular* times.

Definition 8 (Detailed Balance). *A Markov chain with transition matrix $\mathbf{T}$ fulfills the detailed balance condition for a distribution p, iff*

$$p(x)T_{xx'} = p(x')T_{x'x}$$

---

[1]gcd: greatest common divisor

or in the continuous case

$$p(x)T(x'|x) = p(x')T(x|x')$$

holds for all x and x'.

Informally this means that the probability of being in state x and moving to state x' equals the probability of being in state x' and moving back to state x. The detailed balance condition is sufficient to ensure that $p(x)$ is stationary for $\mathbf{T}$ (or T).

Theorem 1 (Detailed Balance). *If $\mathbf{T}$ (or T) satisfies the detailed balance condition for distribution p, then p is stationary distribution of $\mathbf{T}$ (or T).*

Proof.

$$\sum_x p(x)T_{xx'} = \sum_x p(x')T_{x'x} = p(x') \sum_x T_{x'x} = p(x')$$

$$\int p(x)T(x'|x)dx = \int p(x')T(x|x')dx = p(x')$$

$\square$

To illustrate the convergence properties of Markov chains, let us randomly draw 10 points on the probability simplex and perform 30 Markov chain iterations. To provide a more vivid visualization, we interpolate all points using polynomials. We show convergence results on a unit 2-simplex $(\dim(p) = 3)$ in Fig. A.8 and on a unit 3-simplex $(\dim(p) = 4)$ in Fig. A.9. A black square marks the final state of each Markov chain. Stationary distributions are computed from the first eigenvector of $\mathbf{T}$ and depicted as a black circles. For the periodic and reducible case, all chains converge to the sub-simplex of the reduced transition matrix (for the 2-simplex the sub-simplex corresponds to a line), but continue oscillating in this space. Thus no stationary distribution can be found. For the periodic and irreducible example, all chains are orbiting around the center of the simplex and never converge. For the aperiodic and reducible case, all Markov chains converge to a common stationary distribution, but the stationary point is confined to the sub-simplex of the reduced matrix. When the transition matrix is aperiodic and irreducible, all trajectories converge to a stationary distribution, defined by the first eigenvector of **T**.

A.3.3. Combining Kernels

Transition kernels of Markov chains have the nice property that they can be combined by concatenation. This allows for constructing complex moves from simple ones.

Theorem 2 (Kernel Concatenation). *Let T_1 and T_2 be kernels with stationary distribution p. Then $T(x'|x) \equiv \int T_2(x'|\tilde{x})T_1(\tilde{x}|x)d\tilde{x}$ is another transtion kernel with stationary distribution p.*

Proof.

$$
\begin{aligned}
\int T(x'|x)p(x)dx &= \int \int T_2(x'|\tilde{x})T_1(\tilde{x}|x)d\tilde{x}\, p(x)dx \\
&= \int T_2(x'|\tilde{x}) \int T_1(\tilde{x}|x)p(x)dx\, d\tilde{x} \\
&= \int T_2(x'|\tilde{x})p(\tilde{x})d\tilde{x} \\
&= p(x')
\end{aligned}
$$

$\square$

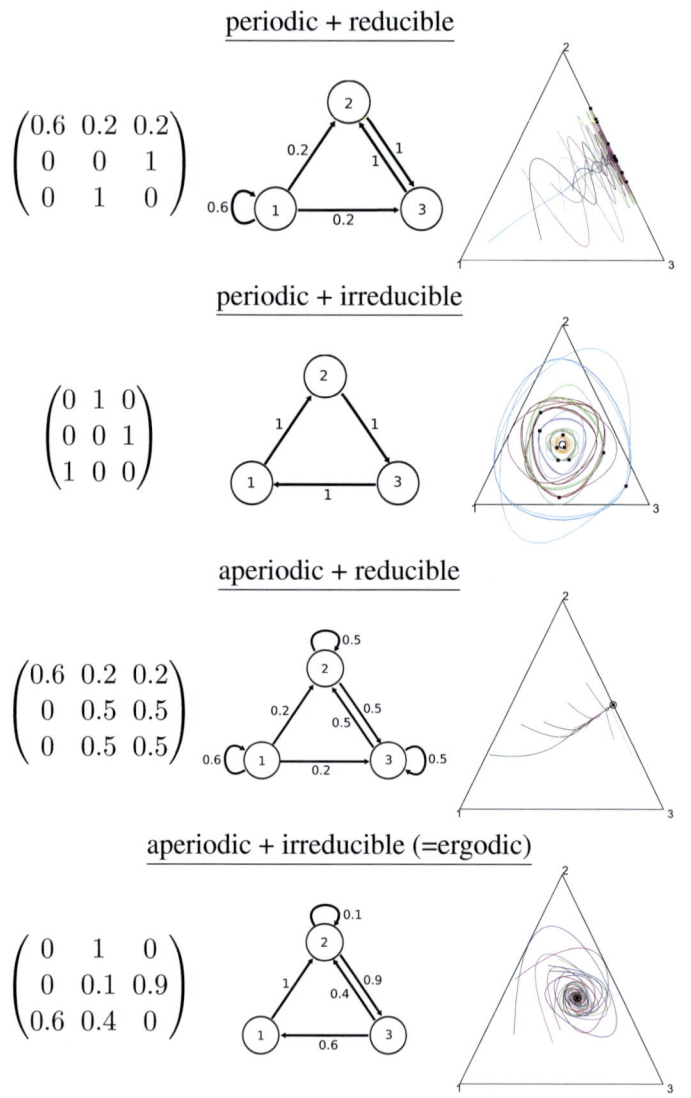

Figure A.8.: **Markov chains on the 2-Simplex.** From left to right: Stochastic transition matrix **T**, transition graph and 10 runs of the process. Squares denote final states after 30 iterations, circles denote stationary states.

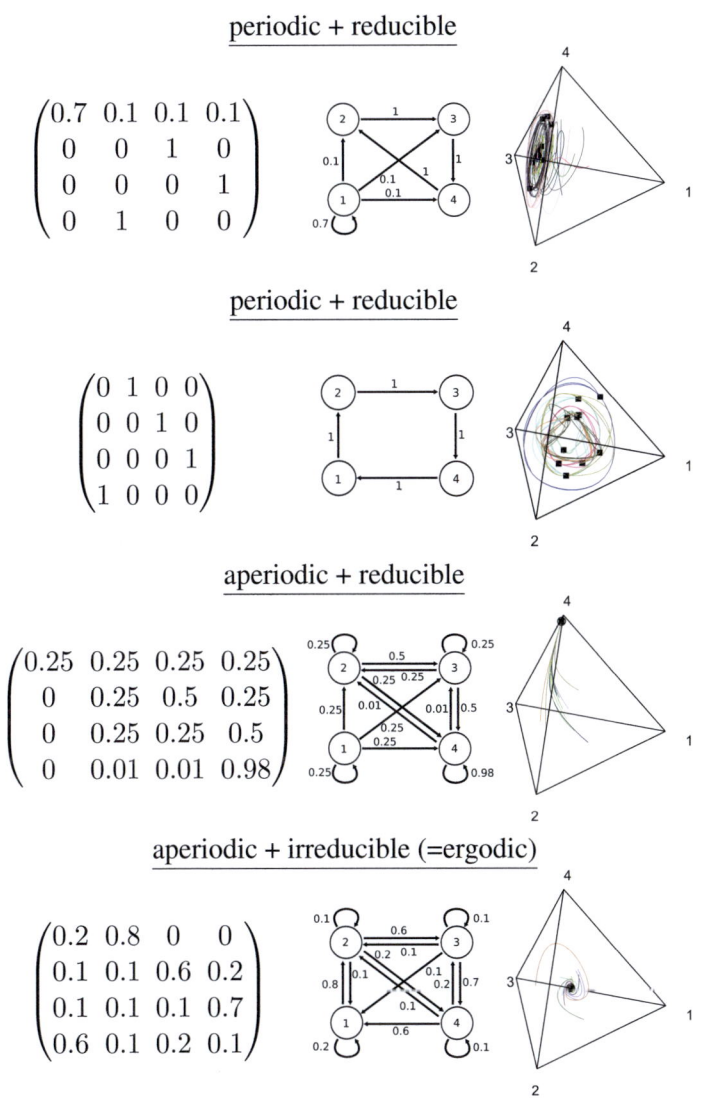

Figure A.9.: **Markov chains on the 3-Simplex.** From left to right: Stochastic transition matrix **T**, transition graph and 10 runs of the process. Squares denote final states after 30 iterations, circles denote stationary states.

Theorem 3 (Kernel Mixing). *Let T_1 and T_2 be transition kernels with stationary distribution p and $w_1, w_2 \geq 0$ with $w_1 + w_2 = 1$. Then $T(x'|x) \equiv w_1 T_1(x'|x) + w_2 T_2(x'|x)$ is another transtion kernel with stationary distribution p.*

Proof.

$$
\begin{aligned}
\int T(x'|x)p(x)dx &= \int \left(w_1 T_1(x'|x) + w_2 T_2(x'|x) \right) p(x)dx \\
&= w_1 p(x') + w_2 p(x') \\
&= p(x')
\end{aligned}
$$

$\square$

A.4. Markov Chain Monte Carlo

To make use of Markov chains for sampling, we need to construct a chain with stationary distribution $p(x)$. This is called the Markov Chain Monte Carlo approach. In contrast to the sampling schemes discussed so far, samples from a Markov chain will be temporally correlated, but for many applications this is not a problem. The first samples we draw will be biased towards the user-specified initial state of the Markov chain and should thus be removed. This stage is often called 'burn-in' phase.

A.4.1. Metropolis-Hastings Sampling

First, we consider the popular Metropolis-Hastings (MH) algorithm, which is very easy to implement and satisfies the detailed balance condition. The idea is to use a proposal distribution q from which samples can be drawn easily and efficiently. Given x, a proposed sample $x' \sim q(x'|x)$ is accepted with probability

$$
p_{MH}(x'|x) = \min \left\{ 1, \frac{p(x')q(x|x')}{p(x)q(x'|x)} \right\} \tag{A.14}
$$

Algorithm 5 Metropolis-Hastings

$x_1 \leftarrow$ initial state
$i \leftarrow 2$
while $i < N$ **do**
$\quad$ draw $x_i \sim q(x_i|x_{i-1})$
$\quad$ draw $u_i \sim \mathcal{U}(0,1)$
$\quad$ **if** $u_i > \frac{p(x_i)q(x_{i-1}|x_i)}{p(x_{i-1})q(x_i|x_{i-1})}$ **then**
$\quad\quad x_i \leftarrow x_{i-1}$
$\quad i \leftarrow i+1$

Informally this means that a proposed state is accepted, if the target density $p(x')$ is high and it is likely to get back to the old state $q(x|x')$ using the next proposal. If a sample x' is accepted, it is added to the Markov chain, otherwise the old state x is added. If q is symmetric Eq. A.14 becomes

$$p_{MH}(x'|x) = \min\left\{1, \frac{p(x')}{p(x)}\right\} \tag{A.15}$$

and the resulting algorithm is called Metropolis sampling. The general Metropolis-Hastings algorithm is summarized in Algorithm 5. To show that p is a stationary distribution of T, let us write down the transition kernel T in terms of the acceptance probability Eq. A.14:

$$\begin{aligned} T(x'|x) &= q(x'|x)p_{MH}(x'|x) \\ &+ \delta(x'-x)\int q(\tilde{x}|x)[1 - p_{MH}(\tilde{x}|x)]d\tilde{x} \end{aligned} \tag{A.16}$$

Informally $T(x'|x)$ is the probability of moving from state x to state x' times the acceptance probability of state x' or the probability of staying at state x because either x was proposed and accepted or any other state has been proposed and rejected.

Theorem 4 (Metropolis-Hastings). *p is stationary distribution of T.*

Proof.

$$
\begin{aligned}
\int T(x'|x)p(x)dx &= \int \min\{p(x)q(x'|x), p(x')q(x|x')\}dx \\
&\quad + \int p(x')q(\tilde{x}|x')[1 - p_{MH}(\tilde{x}|x')]d\tilde{x} \\
&= \int \min\{p(x)q(x'|x), p(x')q(x|x')\}dx \\
&\quad + p(x') \int q(\tilde{x}|x')d\tilde{x} \\
&\quad - \int p(x')q(\tilde{x}|x')p_{MH}(\tilde{x}|x')d\tilde{x} \\
&= \int \min\{p(x)q(x'|x), p(x')q(x|x')\}dx \\
&\quad + p(x') \\
&\quad - \int \min\{p(x')q(\tilde{x}|x'), p(\tilde{x})q(x'|\tilde{x})\}d\tilde{x} \\
&= p(x')
\end{aligned}
$$

$\square$

Let us now turn back to our example of sampling the mean μ and variance σ of a univariate Gaussian. Again, we first sample $N = 50$ data points from $\mathcal{N}(\mu = 0, \sigma = 0.5)$. For sampling $\mathbf{x} = (\mu, \sigma)^{\mathsf{T}}$, we use the Metropolis algorithm with the proposal distribution

$$q(\mathbf{x}'|\mathbf{x}) \sim \mathcal{N}(\mathbf{x}, 0.05\,\mathbf{I}) \tag{A.17}$$

Fig. A.10 shows that the Metropolis sampler has a better acceptance rate than the rejection sampler from Section A.2.2. Unfortunately this rate depends heavily on the particular choice of the proposal distribution q and making the right choice is crucial for applying Metropolis-Hastings to problems of practical relevance. A Markov

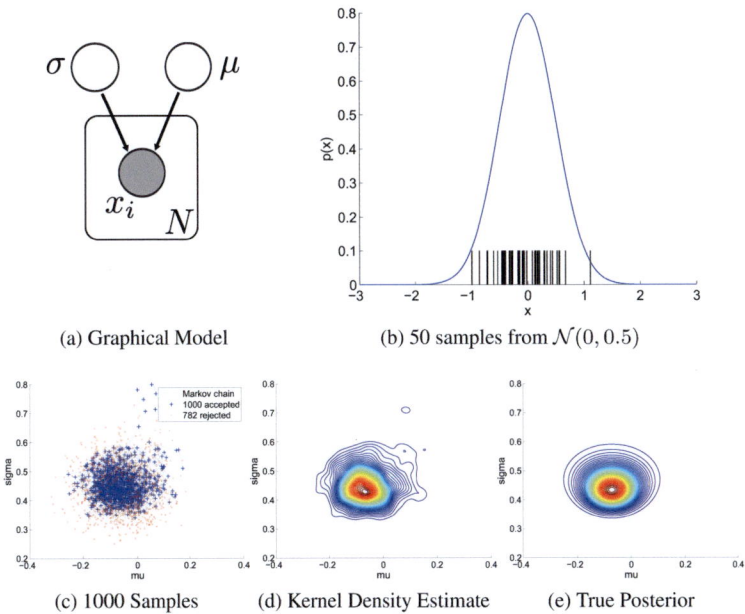

(a) Graphical Model   (b) 50 samples from $\mathcal{N}(0, 0.5)$

(c) 1000 Samples   (d) Kernel Density Estimate   (e) True Posterior

Figure A.10.: **Markov Chain Monte Carlo Sampling.** Given independent samples from a Gaussian distribution we infer the posterior over μ and σ using the Metropolis sampling algorithm with $q(\mathbf{x}'|\mathbf{x}) \sim \mathcal{N}(\mathbf{x}, 0.05\,\mathbf{I})$.

chain that traverses the state space efficiently is said to be *well mixing*. In contrast, a Markov chain that easily gets trapped in small areas of the search space is called *poorly mixing*. The first samples of the chain ('burn-in' samples) are typically rejected from the final estimate.

Let us now reconsider the robot localization problem from Fig. A.5, but this time using the Metropolis algorithm and assuming unknown noise in the distance measurements σ as illustrated in Fig. A.11. Since we are also concerned about estimating the sensor noise σ, we use 16 measurements (instead of only four in the previous example) in order to gain robustness. Again, the prior for the robot's location $\mathbf{x}$ is assumed to be uniformly distributed on the unit square

133

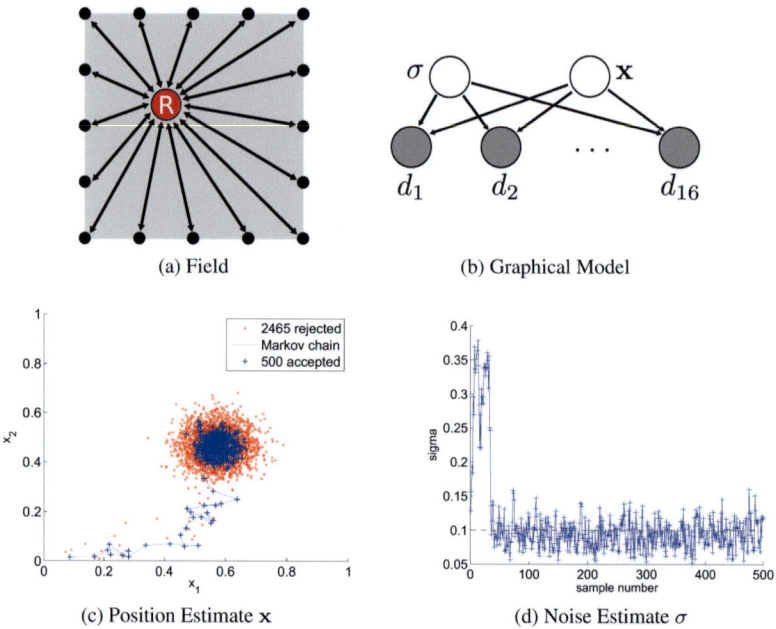

(a) Field

(b) Graphical Model

(c) Position Estimate $\mathbf{x}$

(d) Noise Estimate σ

Figure A.11.: **Robot Localization using the Metropolis Algorithm.** The second row shows the Markov chain for the robot's position $\mathbf{x}$ and the measurement noise σ. The true parameters are $\mathbf{x} = (0.5, 0.5)$ and $\sigma = 0.1$.

and we assume a uniform prior on the interval $[0.01, 0.5]$ for σ, which is now a stochastic variable as well:

$$\mathbf{x} \sim \mathcal{U}([0,1] \times [0,1]) \qquad (A.18)$$

$$\sigma \sim \mathcal{U}(0.01, 0.5) \qquad (A.19)$$

The measurements are modeled using a Gaussian distribution

$$d_i | \mathbf{x}, \sigma \sim \mathcal{N}(\|\mathbf{x} - \mathbf{e}_i\|, \sigma^2) \qquad (A.20)$$

Since all measurements are assumed independent, the posterior of the robot's position given the 16 measurements $\{d_1, ..., d_{16}\}$ is

$$
\begin{aligned}
p(\mathbf{x}, \sigma | d_1, ...d_{16}) &\propto p(\mathbf{x})p(\sigma)p(d_1|\mathbf{x}, \sigma) \cdots p(d_{16}|\mathbf{x}, \sigma) \\
&\propto [0 \le x_1, x_2 \le 1] \times [0.01 \le \sigma \le 0.5] \\
&\times \frac{\exp\left(-\frac{1}{2\sigma^2}\sum_{i=1}^{16}[\|\mathbf{x} - \mathbf{e}_i\| - d_i]^2\right)}{(2\pi\sigma^2)^8}
\end{aligned}
$$

Sampling results with accepted and rejected samples are depicted in Fig. A.11. After a small 'burn-in' period, the mode of the posterior is found in terms of position as well as in terms of noise, while only rejecting a relatively small number of samples.

A.4.2. Gibbs Sampling

When dealing with multivariate posterior distributions, it is also possible to update variables only partly and loop over the updates. One popular and efficient choice of such a cyclic MH kernel is known as Gibbs sampling. The idea in Gibbs sampling is to introduce knowledge about the distributions into the sampling process by adopting full conditional distributions

$$
p(x_k | x_1, ..., x_{k-1}, x_{k+1}, ..., x_D) \tag{A.21}
$$

as proposal distributions for each k. Note that in contrast to the previous section, here x_k denotes the k'th dimension of random vector $\mathbf{x}$ and $\dim(\mathbf{x}) = D$ is its dimensionality. By applying this procedure all samples get accepted, making Gibbs sampling very efficient in practice. However, the conditional posterior must be easy to sample, whereas for Metropolis-Hastings the posterior must only be evaluated up to a multiplicative constant. Note that it is also possible to group variables and sample from grouped conditionals.

In Gibbs sampling, the proposal distribution is chosen as

$$
q(\mathbf{x}'|\mathbf{x}) = p(x_k|\mathbf{x}_{-k})\, \delta(\mathbf{x}'_{-k} - \mathbf{x}_{-k}) \tag{A.22}
$$

135

Algorithm 6 Gibbs sampling

$\mathbf{x}_1 \leftarrow$ initial state
for $i \leftarrow 2$ to N **do**
    for $k \leftarrow 1$ to D **do**
        draw sample $x_i^k \sim p(x_i^k | x_i^1, ..., x_i^{k-1}, x_{i-1}^{k+1}, ..., x_{i-1}^D)$

---

for $k \in \{1, ..., D\}$. Here $\mathbf{x}_{-k}$ denotes all entries of $\mathbf{x}$ without entry k. It is easy to show that all Gibbs moves are accepted using this proposal distribution.

Theorem 5 (Gibbs). *Gibbs moves are accepted with probability* 1.

Proof. As $\mathbf{x}'_{-k} = \mathbf{x}_{-k}$, the acceptance probability becomes

$$
\begin{aligned}
p_{MH}(\mathbf{x}'|\mathbf{x}) &= \min\left\{1, \frac{p(\mathbf{x}')q(\mathbf{x}|\mathbf{x}')}{p(\mathbf{x})q(\mathbf{x}'|\mathbf{x})}\right\} \\
&= \min\left\{1, \frac{p(\mathbf{x}')p(x_k|\mathbf{x}'_{-k})}{p(\mathbf{x})p(x'_k|\mathbf{x}_{-k})}\right\} \\
&= \min\left\{1, \frac{p(x'_k, \mathbf{x}'_{-k})p(x_k|\mathbf{x}'_{-k})}{p(x_k, \mathbf{x}_{-k})p(x'_k|\mathbf{x}_{-k})}\right\} \\
&= \min\left\{1, \frac{p(x'_k|\mathbf{x}'_{-k})p(\mathbf{x}'_{-k})p(x_k|\mathbf{x}'_{-k})}{p(x_k|\mathbf{x}_{-k})p(\mathbf{x}_{-k})p(x'_k|\mathbf{x}_{-k})}\right\} \\
&= \min\{1, 1\} = 1
\end{aligned}
$$

$\square$

Note that the proposal distribution is reducible, since we are not exploiting the full state space. This 'problem' is addressed by sampling several times from different components k of $\mathbf{x}$ (=different dimensions). After a full cycle the sample is added to the list. The full algorithm is given in Algorithm 6.

Let us illustrate Gibbs sampling on our previous example of sampling the posterior parameters of a univariate Gaussian. Note that the simple uniform priors we employed in the other examples cannot

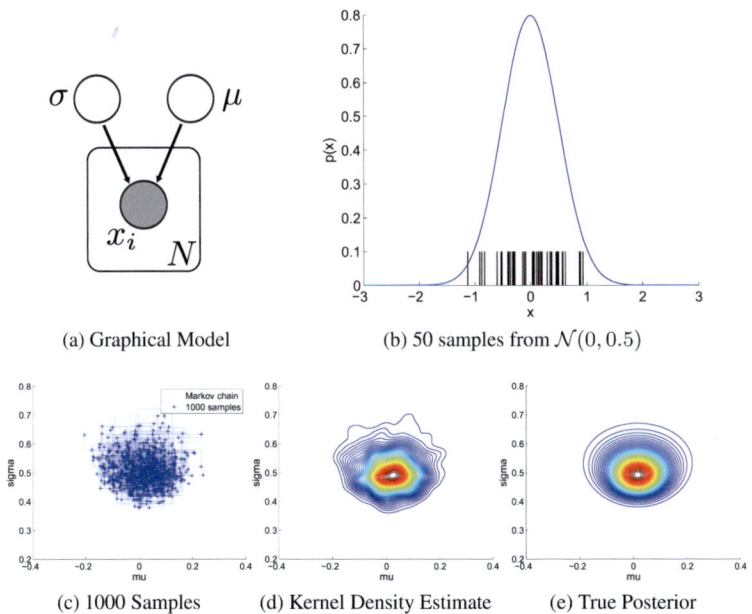

(a) Graphical Model (b) 50 samples from $\mathcal{N}(0, 0.5)$

(c) 1000 Samples (d) Kernel Density Estimate (e) True Posterior

Figure A.12.: **Gibbs Sampling.** Given 50 independent samples from a Gaussian distribution the posterior over μ and σ is sampled using Gibbs sampling. Non-informative priors on μ and σ are assumed.

be used for Gibbs sampling as they lead to non-standard conditional posterior distributions. Instead, we focus on posterior distributions with a well-defined analytical form, for which out-of-the-box samplers can be used. Such posteriors can be obtained by using conjugate priors, which have the same analytical form as the posterior. The only difference is an update on the parameters. It is well known that the conjugate prior for the mean of the Gaussian is Gaussian, and the conjugate prior for the precision (inverse variance) is a Gamma distribution. For details on conjugate priors the reader is referred to [76].

Let us now show that the state conjugacy relationships hold indeed, starting with the Gaussian mean. Instead of working with the

137

variance σ^2 we employ the so-called precision parameter $\lambda = \sigma^{-2}$ for notational simplicity. Assuming that the data likelihood and the prior for the mean μ and precision λ are given by

$$x_i|\mu, \lambda \sim \mathcal{N}(\mu, \lambda^{-1}) \propto \sqrt{\lambda} \exp\left\{ -\frac{\lambda}{2}(x_i - \mu)^2 \right\} \quad (A.23)$$

$$\mu \sim \mathcal{N}(\xi, \kappa^{-1}) \propto \exp\left\{ -\frac{\kappa}{2}(\mu - \xi)^2 \right\} \quad (A.24)$$

$$\lambda \sim \Gamma(\alpha, \beta^{-1}) \propto \lambda^{\alpha-1} \exp\left\{ -\lambda\beta \right\} \quad (A.25)$$

the posterior of μ given λ and the posterior of λ given μ is easily found by completing the square:

$$\mu|x_1, .., x_N, \lambda \sim \mathcal{N}\left(\frac{\lambda \sum_i x_i + \kappa\xi}{\lambda N + \kappa}, (\lambda N + \kappa)^{-1} \right) \quad (A.26)$$

$$\lambda|x_1, .., x_N, \mu \sim \Gamma\left(\alpha + \frac{N}{2}, \left(\frac{1}{2}\sum_i (x_i - \mu)^2 + \beta \right)^{-1} \right) \quad (A.27)$$

The bivariate Gibbs sampler for the posterior of a Gaussian is now readily given by drawing samples alternately from $p(\lambda|x_1, .., x_N, \mu)$ and $p(\mu|x_1, .., x_N, \lambda)$, while keeping the other variable fixed in turn. This is illustrated in Fig. A.12 using uninformative priors with $\xi = \kappa = \alpha = \beta = 0$.

B. Bibliography

[1] P. F. Alcantarilla. *Vision Based Localization: From Humanoid Robots to Visually Impaired People.* PhD thesis, University of Alcala, Alcala de Henares, Madrid, Spain, October 2011.

[2] Y. Alon, A. Ferencz, and A. Shashua. Off-road path following using region classification and geometric projection constraints. In *Proc. IEEE Conf. on Computer Vision and Pattern Recognition (CVPR),* 2006.

[3] J. M. Alvarez, T. Gevers, and A. M. Lopez. 3d scene priors for road detection. In *Proc. IEEE Conf. on Computer Vision and Pattern Recognition (CVPR),* 2010.

[4] M. Aly. Real time detection of lane markers in urban streets. In *Proc. IEEE Intelligent Vehicles Symposium (IV),* 2008.

[5] C. Andrieu, N. de Freitas, A. Doucet, and M. I. Jordan. An introduction to MCMC for machine learning. *Machine Learning,* 50(1-2):5–43, 2003.

[6] M. Andriluka, S. Roth, and B. Schiele. People-tracking-by-detection and people-detection-by-tracking. In *Proc. IEEE Conf. on Computer Vision and Pattern Recognition (CVPR),* 2008.

[7] M. Andriluka, S. Roth, and B. Schiele. Monocular 3d pose estimation and tracking by detection. In *Proc. IEEE Conf. on Computer Vision and Pattern Recognition (CVPR),* 2010.

[8] N. Apostoloff and A. Zelinsky. Robust vision based lane tracking using multiple cues and particle filtering. In *Proc. IEEE Intelligent Vehicles Symposium (IV)*, 2003.

[9] A. Bachmann and I. Lulcheva. Bayesian scene segmentation incorporating motion constraints and category-specific information. In *Proc. of the Conf. on Computer Vision Theory and Applications (VISAPP)*, 2009.

[10] H. Badino, U. Franke, and R. Mester. Free space computation using stochastic occupancy grids and dynamic programming. In *Proc. IEEE International Conf. on Computer Vision (ICCV) Workshops*, 2007.

[11] H. Badino, U. Franke, and D. Pfeiffer. The stixel world - a compact medium level representation of the 3d-world. In *Proc. of the DAGM Symposium on Pattern Recognition (DAGM)*, 2009.

[12] H. Badino, R. Mester, T. Vaudrey, and U. Franke. Stereo-based free space computation in complex traffic scenarios. In *Proc. IEEE Southwest Symposium on Image Analysis and Interpretation*, pages 189–192, March 2008.

[13] M. Bajracharya, B. Moghaddam, A. Howard, S. Brennan, and L. H. Matthies. A fast stereo-based system for detecting and tracking pedestrians from a moving vehicle. *International Journal of Robotics Research (IJRR)*, 28:1466–1485, 2009.

[14] S. Bao, M. Sun, and S. Savarese. Toward coherent object detection and scene layout understanding. In *Proc. IEEE Conf. on Computer Vision and Pattern Recognition (CVPR)*, 2010.

[15] O. Barinova, V. Lempitsky, E. Tretyak, and P. Kohli. Geometric image parsing in man-made environments. In *Proc. of the European Conf. on Computer Vision (ECCV)*, 2010.

[16] E. Baseski and L. Baunegaard. Road interpretation for driver assistance based on an early cognitive vision system. In *Proc. of the Conf. on Computer Vision Theory and Applications (VISAPP)*, 2009.

[17] H. Bay, A. Ess, and L. Tuytelaars, Tinne andVan Gool. Speeded-up robust features (surf). *Computer Vision and Image Understanding (CVIU)*, 110(3):346–359, 2008.

[18] H. Bay, T. Tuytelaars, and L. V. Gool. Surf: Speeded up robust features. In *Proc. of the European Conf. on Computer Vision (ECCV)*, 2006.

[19] R. Benenson, M. Mathias, R. Timofte, and L. J. V. Gool. Pedestrian detection at 100 frames per second. In *Proc. IEEE Conf. on Computer Vision and Pattern Recognition (CVPR)*, 2012.

[20] M. Betke, E. Haritaoglu, and L. S. Davis. Real-time multiple vehicle detection and tracking from a moving vehicle. *Machine Vision and Applications (MVA)*, 12(2):69–83, 2000.

[21] S. M. Bileschi. *StreetScenes: Towards Scene Understanding in Still Images*. PhD thesis, Massachusetts Institute of Technology, 2006.

[22] C. M. Bishop. *Pattern Recognition and Machine Learning*. Springer, 1st ed. 2006 edition, October 2006.

[23] G. Bradski and A. Kaehler. *Learning OpenCV: Computer Vision with the OpenCV Library*. O'Reilly, Cambridge, MA, 2008.

[24] M. D. Breitenstein, F. Reichlin, B. Leibe, E. Koller-Meier, and L. Van Gool. Robust tracking-by-detection using a detector confidence particle filter. In *Proc. IEEE International Conf. on Computer Vision (ICCV)*, 2009.

[25] M. D. Breitenstein, E. Sommerlade, B. Leibe, L. Van Gool, and I. Reid. Probabilistic parameter selection for learning scene structure from video. In *Proc. of the British Machine Vision Conf. (BMVC)*, 2008.

[26] J. E. Bresenham. Algorithm for computer control of a digital plotter. *IBM*, 4(1):25–30, 1965.

[27] A. Broggi. A massively parallel approach to real-time vision-based road markings detection. In *Proc. IEEE Intelligent Vehicles Symposium (IV)*, 1995.

[28] A. Broggi, P. Medici, P. Zani, A. Coati, and M. Panciroli. Autonomous vehicles control in the VisLab Intercontinental Autonomous Challenge. *Annual Reviews in Control*, 36(1):161–171, 2012.

[29] M. A. Brubaker, A. Geiger, and R. Urtasun. Lost! leveraging the crowd for probabilistic visual self-localization. In *Proc. IEEE Conf. on Computer Vision and Pattern Recognition (CVPR)*, 2013.

[30] M. Buehler, K. Iagnemma, and S. Singh. *The 2005 darpa grand challenge: The great robot race*, volume 36. Springer, 2007.

[31] M. Buehler, K. Iagnemma, and S. Singh, editors. *The DARPA Urban Challenge*, volume 56 of *Advanced Robotics*, 2009.

[32] Y. Cai, N. de Freitas, and J. J. Little. Robust visual tracking for multiple targets. In *Proc. of the European Conf. on Computer Vision (ECCV)*, 2006.

[33] M. Calonder, V. Lepetit, M. Ozuysal, T. Trzcinski, C. Strecha, and P. Fua. Brief: Computing a local binary descriptor very fast. *IEEE Trans. on Pattern Analysis and Machine Intelligence (PAMI)*, 34(7):1281–1298, 2012.

[34] M. Calonder, V. Lepetit, C. Strecha, and P. Fua. Brief: Binary robust independent elementary features. In *Proc. of the European Conf. on Computer Vision (ECCV)*, 2010.

[35] J. Canny. A computational approach to edge detection. *IEEE Trans. on Pattern Analysis and Machine Intelligence (PAMI)*, 8(6):679–698, November 1986.

[36] M. Cech. *Fahrspurschätzung aus monokularen Bildfolgen für innerstädtische Fahrerassistenzanwendungen*. PhD thesis, Karlsruhe Institute of Technology, 2009.

[37] W. Choi and S. Savarese. Multiple target tracking in world coordinate with single, minimally calibrated camera. In *Proc. of the European Conf. on Computer Vision (ECCV)*, 2010.

[38] W. Choi and S. Savarese. A unified framework for multi-target tracking and collective activity recognition. In *Proc. of the European Conf. on Computer Vision (ECCV)*, 2012.

[39] N. Chumerin and M. Van Hulle. Ground plane estimation based on dense stereo disparity. In *Proc. of the International Conference on Artificial Intelligence and Neural Networks (ICAINN)*, 2008.

[40] N. Cornelis, B. Leibe, K. Cornelis, and L. J. Van Gool. 3d urban scene modeling integrating recognition and reconstruction. *International Journal of Computer Vision (IJCV)*, 78(2-3):121–141, July 2008.

[41] J. Crisman and C. Thorpe. Scarf: A color vision system that tracks roads and intersections. *IEEE Trans. on Robotics and Automation (TRA)*, 9(1):49–58, February 1993.

[42] H. Dahlkamp, A. Kaehler, D. Stavens, S. Thrun, and G. R. Bradski. Self-supervised monocular road detection in desert terrain. In *Proc. Robotics: Science and Systems (RSS)*, 2006.

[43] H. Dahlkamp, H.-H. Nagel, A. Ottlik, and P. Reuter. A framework for model-based tracking experiments in image sequences. *International Journal of Computer Vision (IJCV)*, 73(2):139–157, 2007.

[44] R. Danescu and S. Nedevschi. Probabilistic lane tracking in difficult road scenarios using stereovision. *IEEE Trans. on Intelligent Transportation Systems (TITS)*, 10(2):272–282, 2009.

[45] R. Danescu, S. Nedevschi, M. M. Meinecke, and T. B. To. Lane geometry estimation in urban environments using a stereovision system. In *Proc. IEEE Conf. on Intelligent Transportation Systems (ITSC)*, 2007.

[46] T. Dang, C. Hoffmann, and C. Stiller. Continuous stereo self-calibration by camera parameter tracking. *IEEE Trans. on Image Processing (TIP)*, 18(7):1536–50, 2009.

[47] A. J. Davison. Real-time simultaneous localization and mapping with a single camera. In *Proc. IEEE International Conf. on Computer Vision (ICCV)*, 2003.

[48] C. De Boor. *A Practical Guide to Splines*. Number 27 in Applied Mathematical Sciences. Springer-Verlag, 1978.

[49] V. Delaitre, D. Fouhey, I. Laptev, J. Sivic, A. Gupta, and A. Efros. Scene semantics from long-term observation of people. In *Proc. of the European Conf. on Computer Vision (ECCV)*, 2012.

[50] C. Desai, D. Ramanan, and C. Fowlkes. Discriminative models for multi-class object layout. In *Proc. IEEE International Conf. on Computer Vision (ICCV)*, 2009.

[51] E. D. Dickmanns and B. D. Mysliwetz. Recursive 3-d road and relative ego-state recognition. *IEEE Trans. on Pattern*

Analysis and Machine Intelligence (PAMI), 14(2):199–213, Feb 1992.

[52] A. H. Dodson, G. V. Moon, T. Moore, and D. Jones. Guiding blind pedestrians with a personal navigation system. *Journal of Navigation*, 52:330–341, 1999.

[53] P. Dollar, S. Belongie, and P. Perona. The fastest pedestrian detector in the west. In *Proc. of the British Machine Vision Conf. (BMVC)*, 2010.

[54] B. A. Draper, R. T. Collins, J. Brolio, A. R. Hanson, and E. M. Riseman. The schema system. *International Journal of Computer Vision (IJCV)*, 2(3):209–250, 1989.

[55] C. Duchow. A novel, signal model based approach to lane detection for use in intersection assistance. In *Proc. IEEE Conf. on Intelligent Transportation Systems (ITSC)*, 2006.

[56] W. Enkelmann, G. Struck, and J. Geisler. Roma - a system for model-based analysis of road markings. In *Proc. IEEE Intelligent Vehicles Symposium (IV)*, 1995.

[57] A. Ess, B. Leibe, K. Schindler, and L. V. Gool. Robust multi-person tracking from a mobile platform. *IEEE Trans. on Pattern Analysis and Machine Intelligence (PAMI)*, 31:1831–1846, 2009.

[58] A. Ess, T. Mueller, H. Grabner, and L. van Gool. Segmentation-based urban traffic scene understanding. In *Proc. of the British Machine Vision Conf. (BMVC)*, 2009.

[59] M. Everingham, L. Van Gool, C. K. I. Williams, J. Winn, and A. Zisserman. The pascal visual object classes (voc) challenge. *International Journal of Computer Vision (IJCV)*, 88(2):303–338, 2010.

[60] P. Felzenszwalb, R. Girshick, D. McAllester, and D. Ramanan. Object detection with discriminatively trained part based models. *IEEE Trans. on Pattern Analysis and Machine Intelligence (PAMI)*, 32:1627–1645, 2010.

[61] P. F. Felzenszwalb, R. B. Girshick, and D. A. McAllester. Cascade object detection with deformable part models. In *Proc. IEEE Conf. on Computer Vision and Pattern Recognition (CVPR)*, 2010.

[62] M. A. Fischler and R. C. Bolles. Random sample consensus: a paradigm for model fitting with applications to image analysis and automated cartography. *Communications of the ACM*, 24:381–395, 1981.

[63] G. Floros and B. Leibe. Joint 2d-3d temporally consistent semantic segmentation of street scenes. In *Proc. IEEE Conf. on Computer Vision and Pattern Recognition (CVPR)*, 2012.

[64] U. Franke and A. Joos. Real-time stereo vision for urban traffic scene understanding. In *Proc. IEEE Intelligent Vehicles Symposium (IV)*, 2000.

[65] D. M. Gavrila and S. Munder. Multi-cue pedestrian detection and tracking from a moving vehicle. *International Journal of Computer Vision (IJCV)*, 73:41–59, 2007.

[66] A. Geiger. Monocular road mosaicing for urban environments. In *Proc. IEEE Intelligent Vehicles Symposium (IV)*, 2009.

[67] A. Geiger and B. Kitt. Objectflow: A descriptor for classifying traffic motion. In *Proc. IEEE Intelligent Vehicles Symposium (IV)*, 2010.

[68] A. Geiger, M. Lauer, F. Moosmann, B. Ranft, H. Rapp, C. Stiller, and J. Ziegler. Team annieway's entry to the grand

cooperative driving challenge 2011. *IEEE Trans. on Intelligent Transportation Systems (TITS)*, 2012.

[69] A. Geiger, M. Lauer, and R. Urtasun. A generative model for 3d urban scene understanding from movable platforms. In *Proc. IEEE Conf. on Computer Vision and Pattern Recognition (CVPR)*, 2011.

[70] A. Geiger, P. Lenz, C. Stiller, and R. Urtasun. Vision meets robotics: The kitti dataset. *International Journal of Robotics Research (IJRR)*, to appear.

[71] A. Geiger, P. Lenz, and R. Urtasun. Are we ready for autonomous driving? The KITTI vision benchmark suite. In *Proc. IEEE Conf. on Computer Vision and Pattern Recognition (CVPR)*, 2012.

[72] A. Geiger, F. Moosmann, O. Car, and B. Schuster. A toolbox for automatic calibration of range and camera sensors using a single shot. In *Proc. IEEE International Conf. on Robotics and Automation (ICRA)*, 2012.

[73] A. Geiger, M. Roser, and R. Urtasun. Efficient large-scale stereo matching. In *Proc. of the Asian Conf. on Computer Vision (ACCV)*, 2010.

[74] A. Geiger, C. Wojek, and R. Urtasun. Joint 3d estimation of objects and scene layout. In *Advances in Neural Information Processing Systems (NIPS)*, 2011.

[75] A. Geiger, J. Ziegler, and C. Stiller. StereoScan: Dense 3d reconstruction in real-time. In *Proc. IEEE Intelligent Vehicles Symposium (IV)*, 2011.

[76] A. Gelman, J. B. Carlin, H. S. Stern, and D. B. Rubin. *Bayesian Data Analysis, Second Edition (Chapman & Hall/CRC Texts in Statistical Science)*. Chapman and Hall/CRC, 2 edition, July 2003.

[77] V. Gengenbach, H. H. Nagel, F. Heimes, G. Struck, and H. Kollnig. Model-based recognition of intersections and lane structures. In *Proc. IEEE Intelligent Vehicles Symposium (IV)*, 1995.

[78] C. J. Geyer. Practical markov chain monte carlo. *Statistical Science*, 7(4):473–483, 1992.

[79] W. Gilks and S. Richardson, editors. *Markov Chain Monte Carlo in Practice*. Chapman & Hall, 1995.

[80] M. Goebl and G. Faerber. A real-time-capable hard- and software architecture for joint image and knowledge processing in cognitive automobiles. In *Proc. IEEE Intelligent Vehicles Symposium (IV)*, 2007.

[81] S. Gould, R. Fulton, and D. Koller. Decomposing a scene into geometric and semantically consistent regions. In *Proc. IEEE International Conf. on Computer Vision (ICCV)*, 2009.

[82] P. J. Green. Reversible jump markov chain monte carlo computation and bayesian model determination. *Biometrika*, 82(4):711–732, 1995.

[83] R. Guo and D. Hoiem. Beyond the line of sight: Labeling the underlying surfaces. In *Proc. of the European Conf. on Computer Vision (ECCV)*, 2012.

[84] A. Gupta, A. A. Efros, and M. Hebert. Blocks world revisited: Image understanding using qualitative geometry and mechanics. In *Proc. of the European Conf. on Computer Vision (ECCV)*, 2010.

[85] R. I. Hartley and A. Zisserman. *Multiple View Geometry in Computer Vision*. Cambridge University Press, second edition, 2004.

[86] W. K. Hastings. Monte carlo sampling methods using markov chains and their applications. *Biometrika*, 57:97–109, 1970.

[87] V. Hedau, D. Hoiem, and D. Forsyth. Recovering the spatial layout of cluttered rooms. In *Proc. IEEE International Conf. on Computer Vision (ICCV)*, 2009.

[88] V. Hedau, D. Hoiem, and D. A. Forsyth. Recovering free space of indoor scenes from a single image. In *Proc. IEEE Conf. on Computer Vision and Pattern Recognition (CVPR)*, 2012.

[89] F. Heimes, K. Fleischer, and H. H. Nagel. Automatic generation of intersection models from digital maps for vision-based driving on inner city intersections. In *Proc. IEEE Intelligent Vehicles Symposium (IV)*, 2000.

[90] F. Heimes and H. H. Nagel. Towards active machine-vision-based driver assistance for urban areas. *International Journal of Computer Vision (IJCV)*, 50(1):5–34, 2002.

[91] G. Heitz, S. Gould, A. Saxena, and D. Koller. Cascaded classification models: Combining models for holistic scene understanding. In *Advances in Neural Information Processing Systems (NIPS)*, 2008.

[92] G. Hinton. Training products of experts by minimizing contrastive divergence. *Neural Computation*, 14:2002, 2000.

[93] H. Hirschmueller. Stereo processing by semiglobal matching and mutual information. *IEEE Trans. on Pattern Analysis and Machine Intelligence (PAMI)*, 30(2):328–341, 2008.

[94] D. Hoiem, A. Efros, and M. Hebert. Putting objects in perspective. In *Proc. IEEE Conf. on Computer Vision and Pattern Recognition (CVPR)*, 2006.

[95] D. Hoiem, A. Efros, and M. Hebert. Putting objects in perspective. *International Journal of Computer Vision (IJCV)*, 80:3–15, 2008.

[96] D. Hoiem, A. A. Efros, and M. Hebert. Geometric context from a single image. In *Proc. IEEE International Conf. on Computer Vision (ICCV)*, 2005.

[97] D. Hoiem, A. A. Efros, and M. Hebert. Recovering surface layout from an image. *International Journal of Computer Vision (IJCV)*, 75(1):151–172, October 2007.

[98] D. Hoiem, A. A. Efros, and M. Hebert. Closing the loop on scene interpretation. In *Proc. IEEE Conf. on Computer Vision and Pattern Recognition (CVPR)*, 2008.

[99] R. Horaud and F. Dornaika. Hand-eye calibration. *International Journal of Robotics Research (IJRR)*, 14(3):195–210, 1995.

[100] A. S. Huang, D. Moore, M. Antone, E. Olson, and S. Teller. Finding multiple lanes in urban road networks with vision and lidar. *Autonomous Robots*, 26(2-3):103–122, 2009.

[101] C. Huang, B. Wu, and R. Nevatia. Robust object tracking by hierarchical association of detection responses. In *Proc. of the European Conf. on Computer Vision (ECCV)*, 2008.

[102] B. Hummel, W. Thiemann, and I. Lulcheva. Description logic for intersection understanding. In *Cognitive Systems with Interactive Sensors (COGIS)*, 2007.

[103] B. Hummel, Z. Yang, and C. Duchow. Kreuzungsverstehen - Ein wissensbasierter Ansatz. *IT*, 49(1):5, 2007.

[104] T. M. Jochem, D. A. Pomerleau, and C. E. Thorpe. Vision based intersection navigation. In *Proc. IEEE Intelligent Vehicles Symposium (IV)*, 1996.

[105] R. E. Kalman. A new approach to linear filtering and prediction problems. *Journal of Basic Engineering (JBE)*, 1(82):35–45, 1960.

[106] S. Kammel, J. Ziegler, and C. Stiller. Team annieway's autonomous system for the 2007 darpa urban challenge. *Journal of Field Robotics (JFR)*, 25(9):615–639, September 2008.

[107] V. Kastrinaki. A survey of video processing techniques for traffic applications. *Image and Vision Computing (IVC)*, 21(4):359, 2003.

[108] R. Kaucic, A. Perera, G. Brooksby, J. Kaufhold, and A. Hoogs. A unified framework for tracking through occlusions and across sensor gaps. In *Proc. IEEE Conf. on Computer Vision and Pattern Recognition (CVPR)*, 2005.

[109] Z. Khan, T. Balch, and F. Dellaert. Mcmc-based particle filtering for tracking a variable number of interacting targets. *IEEE Trans. on Pattern Analysis and Machine Intelligence (PAMI)*, 27(11):1805–1819, 2005.

[110] B. Kitt, A. Geiger, and H. Lategahn. Visual odometry based on stereo image sequences with ransac-based outlier rejection scheme. In *Proc. IEEE Intelligent Vehicles Symposium (IV)*, 2010.

[111] D. Koller, Q. T. Luong, and J. Malik. Using binocular stereopsis for vision-based vehicle control. In *Proc. IEEE Intelligent Vehicles Symposium (IV)*, 1995.

[112] D. Koller, J. Weber, and J. Malik. Towards realtime visual based tracking in cluttered traffic scenes. In *Proc. IEEE Intelligent Vehicles Symposium (IV)*, 1994.

[113] K. Konolige. Small vision system. hardware and implementation. In *Proc. of the International Symposium on Robotics Research (ISRR)*, 1997.

[114] J. Kosecka and W. Zhang. Video compass. In *Proc. of the European Conf. on Computer Vision (ECCV)*, 2002.

[115] D. Kuettel, M. D. Breitenstein, L. V. Gool, and V. Ferrari. What's going on?: Discovering spatio-temporal dependencies in dynamic scenes. In *Proc. IEEE Conf. on Computer Vision and Pattern Recognition (CVPR)*, 2010.

[116] H. W. Kuhn. The Hungarian method for the assignment problem. *Naval Research Logistics Quarterly*, 2:83–97, 1955.

[117] S. Kumar and M. Hebert. Discriminative random fields: A discriminative framework for contextual interaction in classification. In *Proc. IEEE International Conf. on Computer Vision (ICCV)*, pages 1150–1157, 2003.

[118] S. Kumar and M. Hebert. Man-made structure detection in natural images using a causal multiscale random field. In *Proc. IEEE Conf. on Computer Vision and Pattern Recognition (CVPR)*, 2003.

[119] S. Kumar and M. Hebert. A hierarchical field framework for unified context-based classification. In *Proc. IEEE International Conf. on Computer Vision (ICCV)*, 2005.

[120] L. Ladicky, P. Sturgess, C. Russell, S. Sengupta, Y. Bastanlar, W. Clocksin, and P. Torr. Joint optimisation for object class segmentation and dense stereo reconstruction. In *Proc. of the British Machine Vision Conf. (BMVC)*, 2010.

[121] H. Lategahn, A. Geiger, and B. Kitt. Visual slam for autonomous ground vehicles. In *Proc. IEEE International Conf. on Robotics and Automation (ICRA)*, 2011.

[122] H. Lategahn, A. Geiger, B. Kitt, and C. Stiller. Motion-without-structure: Real-time multipose optimization for accurate visual odometry. In *Proc. IEEE Intelligent Vehicles Symposium (IV)*, 2012.

[123] M. Lauer. *Entwicklung eines Monte-Carlo-Verfahrens zum selbstaendigen Lernen von Gauss-Mischverteilungen*. PhD thesis, Universitaet Karlsruhe (TH), 2004.

[124] L. Leal-Taixe, G. Pons-Moll, and B. Rosenhahn. Everybody needs somebody: modeling social and grouping behavior on a linear programming multiple people tracker. In *Proc. IEEE International Conf. on Computer Vision (ICCV) Workshops*, 2011.

[125] D. Lee, A. Gupta, M. Hebert, and T. Kanade. Estimating spatial layout of rooms using volumetric reasoning about objects and surfaces. In *Advances in Neural Information Processing Systems (NIPS)*, 2010.

[126] D. C. Lee, M. Hebert, and T. Kanade. Geometric reasoning for single image structure recovery. In *Proc. IEEE Conf. on Computer Vision and Pattern Recognition (CVPR)*, 2009.

[127] J. Lee. A machine vision system for lane-departure detection. *Computer Vision and Image Understanding (CVIU)*, 86(1):52–78, 2002.

[128] B. Leibe, N. Cornelis, K. Cornelis, and L. Van Gool. Integrating recognition and reconstruction for cognitive traffic scene analysis from a moving vehicle. In *Proc. of the DAGM Symposium on Pattern Recognition (DAGM)*, 2006.

[129] B. Leibe, N. Cornelis, K. Cornelis, and L. Van Gool. Dynamic 3d scene analysis from a moving vehicle. In *Proc. IEEE Conf. on Computer Vision and Pattern Recognition (CVPR)*, 2007.

[130] B. Leibe, K. Schindler, N. Cornelis, and L. Van Gool. Coupled detection and tracking from static cameras and moving vehicles. *IEEE Trans. on Pattern Analysis and Machine Intelligence (PAMI)*, 30(10):1683–1698, 2008.

[131] P. Lenz, J. Ziegler, A. Geiger, and M. Roser. Sparse scene flow segmentation for moving object detection in urban environments. In *Proc. IEEE Intelligent Vehicles Symposium (IV)*, 2011.

[132] S. Leutenegger, M. Chli, and R. Siegwart. Brisk: Binary robust invariant scalable keypoints. In *Proc. IEEE International Conf. on Computer Vision (ICCV)*, pages 2548–2555, 2011.

[133] C.-K. Liang, C.-C. Cheng, Y.-C. Lai, L.-G. Chen, and H. H. Chen. Hardware-efficient belief propagation. In *Proc. IEEE Conf. on Computer Vision and Pattern Recognition (CVPR)*, 2009.

[134] D. G. Lowe. Object recognition from local scale-invariant features. In *Proc. IEEE International Conf. on Computer Vision (ICCV)*, 1999.

[135] D. G. Lowe. Distinctive image features from scale-invariant keypoints. *International Journal of Computer Vision (IJCV)*, 60(2):91–110, 2004.

[136] M. Lutzeler and E. D. Dickmanns. Ems-vision: recognition of intersections on unmarked road networks. In *Proc. IEEE Intelligent Vehicles Symposium (IV)*, 2000.

[137] J. C. McCall and M. M. Trivedi. Video-based lane estimation and tracking for driver assistance: survey, system, and evaluation. *IEEE Trans. on Intelligent Transportation Systems (TITS)*, 7(1):20–37, March 2006.

[138] F. P. McKenna. The human factor in driving accidents an overview of approaches and problems. *Ergonomics*, 25(10):867–877, 1982.

[139] M. Montemerlo, J. Becker, and S. Thrun. Junior: The stanford entry in the urban challenge. *Journal of Field Robotics (JFR)*, 25(9):569–597, September 2008.

[140] K. Mueck. *Rechnergestuetzte Erkennung und Beschreibung innerstaedtischer. Strassenkreuzungen*. PhD thesis, Karlsruhe Institute of Technology (KIT), 2000.

[141] K. Murphy, A. Torralba, and W. T. Freeman. Using the forest to see the trees: A graphical model relating features, objects, and scenes. In *Advances in Neural Information Processing Systems (NIPS)*, 2003.

[142] V. Nedovic, A. W. M. Smeulders, A. Redert, and J. M. Geusebroek. Stages as models of scene geometry. *IEEE Trans. on Pattern Analysis and Machine Intelligence (PAMI)*, 32:1673–1687, 2010.

[143] A. Neubeck and L. V. Gool. Efficient non-maximum suppression. In *Proc. of the International Conf. on Pattern Recognition (ICPR)*, August 2006.

[144] D. Nister, O. Naroditsky, and J. R. Bergen. Visual odometry. In *Proc. IEEE Conf. on Computer Vision and Pattern Recognition (CVPR)*, 2004.

[145] A. Oliva and A. Torralba. Modeling the shape of the scene: a holistic representation of the spatial envelope. *International Journal of Computer Vision (IJCV)*, 42:145–175, 2001.

[146] R. O'Toole. *Gridlock: Why We're Stuck in Traffic and What to Do About It.* 2009.

[147] F. Paetzold, U. Franke, and W. Von Seelen. Lane recognition in urban environment using optimal control theory. In *Proc. IEEE Intelligent Vehicles Symposium (IV)*, 2000.

[148] S. Pellegrini, A. Ess, K. Schindler, and L. J. V. Gool. You'll never walk alone: Modeling social behavior for multi-target tracking. In *Proc. IEEE International Conf. on Computer Vision (ICCV)*, 2009.

[149] L. D. Pero, J. Bowdish, D. Fried, B. Kermgard, E. Hartley, and K. Barnard. Bayesian geometric modeling of indoor scenes. In *Proc. IEEE Conf. on Computer Vision and Pattern Recognition (CVPR)*, 2012.

[150] J. Pilet, A. Geiger, P. Lagger, V. Lepetit, and P. Fua. An all-in-one solution to geometric and photometric calibration. In *Proc. of the International Symposium on Mixed and Augmented Reality (ISMAR)*, 2006.

[151] M. Pollefeys. Detailed real-time urban 3d reconstruction from video. *International Journal of Computer Vision (IJCV)*, 78(2-3):143–167, July 2008.

[152] D. Pomerleau. Ralph: Rapidly adapting lateral position handler. In *Proc. IEEE Intelligent Vehicles Symposium (IV)*, pages 506–511, 1995.

[153] D. Ramanan and D. Forsyth. Finding and tracking people from the bottom up. In *Proc. IEEE Conf. on Computer Vision and Pattern Recognition (CVPR)*, 2003.

[154] C. Rasmussen. Road shape classification for detecting and negotiating intersections. In *Proc. IEEE Intelligent Vehicles Symposium (IV)*, 2003.

[155] L. G. Roberts. *Machine perception of three-dimensional solids*. PhD thesis, Massachusetts Institute of Technology. Dept. of Electrical Engineering, 1963.

[156] S. Roth. *High-Order Markov Random Fields for Low-Level Vision*. PhD thesis, Brown University, 2007.

[157] C. Rother. A new approach for vanishing point detection in architectural environments. In *Proc. of the British Machine Vision Conf. (BMVC)*, 2000.

[158] E. Rublee, V. Rabaud, K. Konolige, and G. Bradski. Orb: an efficient alternative to sift or surf. In *Proc. IEEE International Conf. on Computer Vision (ICCV)*, pages 2564–2571, 2011.

[159] B. Russell, A. Torralba, C. Liu, R. Fergus, and W. Freeman. Object recognition by scene alignment. In *Advances in Neural Information Processing Systems (NIPS)*, 2008.

[160] B. Russell, A. Torralba, K. Murphy, and W. Freeman. Labelme: A database and web-based tool for image annotation. *International Journal of Computer Vision (IJCV)*, 77:157–173, 2008.

[161] A. Saxena, S. H. Chung, and A. Y. Ng. 3-D depth reconstruction from a single still image. *International Journal of Computer Vision (IJCV)*, 76:53–69, 2008.

[162] A. Saxena, J. Schulte, and A. Y. Ng. Depth estimation using monocular and stereo cues. In *Proc. of the International Joint Conf. on Artificial Intelligence (IJCAI)*, 2007.

[163] A. Saxena, M. Sun, and A. Y. Ng. Learning 3-d scene structure from a single still image. In *Proc. IEEE International Conf. on Computer Vision (ICCV)*, 2007.

[164] A. Saxena, M. Sun, and A. Y. Ng. Make3d: Learning 3d scene structure from a single still image. *IEEE Trans. on Pattern Analysis and Machine Intelligence (PAMI)*, 31:824–840, 2009.

[165] D. Scharstein and R. Szeliski. A taxonomy and evaluation of dense two-frame stereo correspondence algorithms. *International Journal of Computer Vision (IJCV)*, 47:7–42, 2002.

[166] G. Schindler and F. Dellaert. Atlanta world: An expectation maximization framework for simultaneous low-level edge

grouping and camera calibration in complex man-made environments. In *Proc. IEEE Conf. on Computer Vision and Pattern Recognition (CVPR)*, 2004.

[167] D. Schulz, W. Burgard, D. Fox, and A. Cremers. People tracking with mobile robots using sample-based joint probabilistic data association filters. *International Journal of Robotics Research (IJRR)*, 22(2):99–116, 2003.

[168] A. Schwing and R. Urtasun. Efficient exact inference for 3d indoor scene understanding. In *Proc. of the European Conf. on Computer Vision (ECCV)*, 2012.

[169] S. Se and M. Brady. Ground plane estimation, error analysis and applications. *Robotics and Autonomous Systems (RAS)*, 39(2):59–71, 2002.

[170] J. Shotton, J. Winn, C. Rother, and A. Criminisi. Textonboost for image understanding: Multi-class object recognition and segmentation by jointly modeling texture, layout, and context. *International Journal of Computer Vision (IJCV)*, 81:2–23, 2009.

[171] N. Silberman, D. Hoiem, P. Kohli, and R. Fergus. Indoor segmentation and support inference from rgbd images. In *Proc. of the European Conf. on Computer Vision (ECCV)*, 2012.

[172] X. Song, J. Cui, H. Zha, and H. Zhao. Vision-based multiple interacting targets tracking via on-line supervised learning. In *Proc. of the European Conf. on Computer Vision (ECCV)*, 2008.

[173] B. Southall and C. J. Taylor. Stochastic road shape estimation. In *Proc. IEEE International Conf. on Computer Vision (ICCV)*, 2001.

[174] P. Sturgess, K. Alahari, L. Ladicky, and P. Torr. Combining appearance and structure from motion features for road scene understanding. In *Proc. of the British Machine Vision Conf. (BMVC)*, 2009.

[175] E. B. Sudderth, A. Torralba, W. T. Freeman, and A. S. Willsky. Describing visual scenes using transformed objects and parts. *International Journal of Computer Vision (IJCV)*, 77(1-3):291–330, 2008.

[176] A. Takahashi and Y. Ninomiya. Model-based lane recognition. In *Proc. IEEE Intelligent Vehicles Symposium (IV)*, 1996.

[177] C. J. Taylor, J. Malik, and J. Weber. A real-time approach to stereopsis and lane-finding. In *Proc. IEEE Intelligent Vehicles Symposium (IV)*, 1996.

[178] S. Thrun, W. Burgard, and D. Fox. *Probabilistic Robotics*. The MIT Press, 2005.

[179] A. Torralba. Contextual priming for object detection. *International Journal of Computer Vision (IJCV)*, 53(2):169–191, 2003.

[180] A. Torralba, K. P. Murphy, and W. T. Freeman. Sharing features: efficient boosting procedures for multiclass object detection. In *Proc. IEEE Conf. on Computer Vision and Pattern Recognition (CVPR)*, 2004.

[181] Z. Tu, X. Chen, A. Yuille, and S. Zhu. Image parsing: Unifying segmentation, detection, and recognition. *International Journal of Computer Vision (IJCV)*, 63(2):113–140, 2005.

[182] M. Vorlander. *Auralization: fundamentals of acoustics, modelling, simulation, algorithms and acoustic virtual reality*. Springer, 2007.

[183] H. Wang, S. Gould, and D. Koller. Discriminative learning with latent variables for cluttered indoor scene understanding. In *Proc. of the European Conf. on Computer Vision (ECCV)*, 2010.

[184] X. Wang, X. Ma, and W. Grimson. Unsupervised activity perception in crowded and complicated scenes using hierarchical bayesian models. *IEEE Trans. on Pattern Analysis and Machine Intelligence (PAMI)*, 31:539–555, 2009.

[185] Y. Wang, L. Bai, and M. Fairhurst. Robust road modeling and tracking using condensation. *IEEE Trans. on Intelligent Transportation Systems (TITS)*, 9(4):570–579, 2008.

[186] J. Weber, D. Koller, Q. T. Luong, and J. Malik. New results in stereo-based automatic vehicle guidance. In *Proc. IEEE Intelligent Vehicles Symposium (IV)*, 1995.

[187] S. Widodo, T. Hasegawa, and S. Tsugawa. Vehicle fuel consumption and emission estimation in environment-adaptive driving with or without inter-vehicle communications. In *Proc. IEEE Intelligent Vehicles Symposium (IV)*, 2000.

[188] Wikipedia. Google driverless car — Wikipedia, the free encyclopedia, 2012. [Online; accessed 06-December-2012].

[189] H. Winner, S. Hakuli, and G. Wolf. *Handbuch Fahrerassistenzsysteme*. Vieweg + Teubner, 2009.

[190] C. Wojek, S. Roth, K. Schindler, and B. Schiele. Monocular 3d scene modeling and inference: Understanding multi-object traffic scenes. In *Proc. of the European Conf. on Computer Vision (ECCV)*, 2010.

[191] C. Wojek and B. Schiele. A dynamic conditional random field model for joint labeling of object and scene classes. In *Proc. of the European Conf. on Computer Vision (ECCV)*, 2008.

[192] C. Wojek, S. Walk, S. Roth, and B. Schiele. Monocular 3d scene understanding with explicit occlusion reasoning. In *Proc. IEEE Conf. on Computer Vision and Pattern Recognition (CVPR)*, 2011.

[193] C. Wojek, S. Walk, S. Roth, K. Schindler, and B. Schiele. Monocular visual scene understanding: Understanding multi-object traffic scenes. *IEEE Trans. on Pattern Analysis and Machine Intelligence (PAMI)*, 2012.

[194] B. Wu and R. Nevatia. Detection and tracking of multiple, partially occluded humans by bayesian combination of edgelet part detectors. *International Journal of Computer Vision (IJCV)*, 75(2):247–266, 2007.

[195] J. Xiao, B. C. Russell, and A. Torralba. Localizing 3d cuboids in single-view images. In *Advances in Neural Information Processing Systems (NIPS)*, December 2012.

[196] K. Yamaguchi, A. C. Berg, L. E. Ortiz, and T. L. Berg. Who are you with and where are you going? In *Proc. IEEE Conf. on Computer Vision and Pattern Recognition (CVPR)*, 2011.

[197] Q. Yu and G. Medioni. Multiple-target tracking by spatiotemporal monte carlo markov chain data association. *IEEE Trans. on Pattern Analysis and Machine Intelligence (PAMI)*, 31(12):2196–2210, 2009.

[198] B. Zcisl, C. Zach, and M. Pollefeys. Stereo reconstruction of building interiors with a vertical structure prior. In *THREED-IMPVT*, 2011.

[199] J. Zhang and H. H. Nagel. Texture-based segmentation of road images. In *Proc. IEEE Intelligent Vehicles Symposium (IV)*, 1994.

[200] L. Zhang, Y. Li, and R. Nevatia. Global data association for multi-object tracking using network flows. In *Proc. IEEE Conf. on Computer Vision and Pattern Recognition (CVPR)*, 2008.

[201] J. Zhao, J. Katupitiya, and J. Ward. Global correlation based ground plane estimation using v-disparity image. In *Proc. IEEE International Conf. on Robotics and Automation (ICRA)*, 2007.

[202] T. Zhao and R. Nevatia. Tracking multiple humans in crowded environment. In *Proc. IEEE Conf. on Computer Vision and Pattern Recognition (CVPR)*, 2004.

[203] L. Zhu, Y. Chen, Y. Lin, C. Lin, and A. Yuille. Recursive segmentation and recognition templates for 2d parsing. In *Advances in Neural Information Processing Systems (NIPS)*, pages 1985–1992, 2009.

Schriftenreihe
Institut für Mess- und Regelungstechnik
Karlsruher Institut für Technologie
(1613-4214)

Die Bände sind unter www.ksp.kit.edu als PDF frei verfügbar oder als Druckausgabe bestellbar.

Band 001   Hans, Annegret
Entwicklung eines Inline-Viskosimeters auf Basis eines
magnetisch-induktiven Durchflussmessers. 2004
ISBN 3-937300-02-3

Band 002   Heizmann, Michael
Auswertung von forensischen Riefenspuren mittels
automatischer Sichtprüfung. 2004
ISBN 3-937300-05-8

Band 003   Herbst, Jürgen
Zerstörungsfreie Prüfung von Abwasserkanälen mit
Klopfschall. 2004
ISBN 3-937300-23-6

Band 004   Kammel, Sören
Deflektometrische Untersuchung spiegelnd
reflektierender Freiformflächen. 2005
ISBN 3-937300-28-7

Band 005   Geistler, Alexander
Bordautonome Ortung von Schienenfahrzeugen mit
Wirbelstrom-Sensoren. 2007
ISBN 978-3-86644-123-1

Band 006   Horn, Jan
Zweidimensionale Geschwindigkeitsmessung
texturierter Oberflächen mit flächenhaften
bildgebenden Sensoren. 2007
ISBN 978-3-86644-076-0

Band 025   Geiger, Andreas
Probabilistic Models for 3D Urban Scene
Understanding from Movable Platforms. 2013
ISBN 978-3-7315-0081-0